FORESHADOWING IN LOPE DE VEGA'S THEATRE

Sonia Harrison Jones

FORESHADOWING IN LOPE DE VEGA'S THEATRE

EP

Erser & Pond

Published in Canada by Erser & Pond Publishers, Ltd.
1096 Queen St., Suite 225, Halifax, N.S., Canada B3H 2R9

Cover design by Benjamin Beaumont
Cover photo ©iStockphoto/Zhenikeyev

Library and Archives Canada Cataloguing in Publication

Jones, Sonia, author
    Foreshadowing in Lope de Vega's theatre / Sonia Harrison Jones.

Based on author's thesis.
Includes bibliographical references.
ISBN 978-1-927883-02-0 (pbk.)

    1. Vega, Lope de, 1562-1635--Criticism and interpretation.
I. Title.

PQ6485.J65 2014   862'.3   C2014-902249-2

This book is dedicated to
two great Hispanists:
José F. Montesinos
and Stephen Gilman.
In memoriam.

To turn your face from clear proofs of deceit,
to drink poison as if it were a soothing liquor,
to disregard gain and delight in being injured,
to believe that heaven can lie contained in hell,
to devote your life and soul to being disillusioned,
this is love; whoever has tasted it, knows.

—LOPE DE VEGA

ACKNOWLEDGMENTS

It would be tedious and difficult for any student to write a PhD dissertation without the warmth and encouragement of professors and mentors who are acquainted with the problems that invariably turn up during such an undertaking. I am very fortunate to have been guided and advised by one of the most inspiring professors I know, my PhD dissertation director Stephen Gilman at Harvard University. I am thankful for the many hours he spent reading and rereading this publication, and for the helpful suggestions made to me by my second reader, Raimundo Lida. I am also especially grateful for the lively, unforgettable discussions I had with José F. Montesinos, my close friend and wise mentor at Bennington College during the quiet summers we spent there with his wife, Nora. "Monte" was also my professor in the M.A. program at the University of California at Berkeley, from which emerged many ideas about love in the life and works of Lope de Vega. I am also very grateful to Yakov Malkiel, my linguistics professor at Berkeley, who taught me to appreciate several languages on their deepest, most subtle levels. These four gifted, highly intelligent scholars are no longer with us, but I shall always remember them with the deepest affection and gratitude.

TABLE OF CONTENTS

Lope de Vega.

INTRODUCTION

The Uses of Foreshadowing

Despite what he might have said in his *Arte Nuevo*,[1] Lope de Vega has often seen fit to let the audience foresee the outcome of his plays. In many of his serious dramas the characters are tormented by visions and omens, they speak with ghosts or hear strange voices, or astrologers give solemn predictions about future events, yet the audience never left the theatre before the play was over. On the contrary, Lope's technique of foreshadowing served to involve the spectators even more in the drama that they saw unfolding before them. Their knowledge of what was in store for the characters served to heighten the suspense, and if the action was of a tragic nature, they watched in fascination as the hero met his inevitable doom. Lope was doubtless aware, too, that the spectators thoroughly enjoyed being let into the secret, for it gave them a feeling of superiority over the characters who doggedly kept striving, despite repeated warnings, to achieve a purpose that would certainly lead to their ultimate downfall.

Lope did not limit himself, however, to the more obvious uses of foreshadowing mentioned above (omens, dreams,

---

[1] *El Arte Nuevo de hacer comedias en este tiempo,* or "The New Art of Writing Plays in this Day and Age" (henceforeward to be referred to as "*El Arte Nuevo*"), is an essay written in verse by Lope de Vega, who read it aloud before the *Academia de Madrid* in 1609, when he explained how he wished to incorporate the best of classical theatre with the new style of the modern, popular Spanish "*Comedia*".

astrologers, voices, ghosts and the like). In most of his plays there is a more fundamental use of foreshadowing based on the traditional themes that were used for plot material. Such themes are found in his historical plays, ballad plays, epic, biblical and mythological plays and others whose subject matter was well known to the spectators. Both author and audience knew in advance the outcome of these plays, and they were able to view the action from an ironic distance which allowed them to see farther and more clearly than the characters themselves.

It cannot be said, however, that Lope's characters were all completely ignorant of their motives and likely destinies. Once in a while Lope created a character who seemed to have an intriguing self-awareness that made him behave as if he himself were infected by the audience's knowledge of what lay ahead. In most cases the devices of foreshadowing (omens, dreams, etc.) were used to point out more specifically the underlying feelings of pessimism and doom in the protagonist who dimly foresaw his fate. Examples of such devices will be found throughout this book. Suffice it to mention such characters as King Sancho in *El príncipe despeñado* ("The Prince Who was Hurled From a Cliff"), who was warned by omens that his majordomo would betray him, or Euridice's accurate foreknowledge in *El marido más firme* ("The Most Steadfast Husband"), or Caupolicán's realization that he would be defeated by the Spaniards in *El Arauco domado* ("The Araucan Tamed").

In these cases the characters are fulfilling a destiny that the audience recognizes as stemming from historical, mythological and epic themes. The spectators see them as the victims of a sort of literary predestination, but because the characters (warned by the various devices of foreshadowing) also share to some extent the foreknowledge of the spectators, they cannot be considered either innocent or pathetic— this would be possible only if they were completely ignorant of their roles and their destinies. Their awareness of what lies ahead, however, forces them into a dramatic situation based on the conflict between their desires and their knowledge of the inevitable consequences of pursuing or fulfilling those desires. The best examples of characters such as these are King Otón in *La Imperial de Otón* ("The Empire of Othon") and Don Alonso in *El caballero de Olmedo* ("The Knight of Olmedo").

The characters that will concern us in this publication, then, are always forewarned by something akin to a "voice of fate". That they are invariably deaf to this voice does not mean they are unaware of its warning; they simply refuse to acknowledge what they have heard, or they conveniently misinterpret the message. They are driven by a passion far stronger than the restrictive and monotonous words of good judgment or common sense: instead, pride drives them to seek revenge, ambition makes them long to wage an unjust war, erotic desire moves them to court an unobtainable lady, or jealousy will lead to their eventual downfall. Many of the characters are heroes with a tragic flaw, but heroes just the same in their battle against the rational world whose rules they understand but cannot, or will not, accept.

Special attention will be given to those plays whose protagonists are particularly affected by the so-called voice of fate. We shall examine the conflicts that arise as a result of their conscience, we shall try to ascertain how their fore-knowledge affects their decisions and actions, and we shall study, in sum, how this self-awareness changes or modifies their own free will, the behavior of the characters around them, and the outcome of the play.

Less attention shall be given to the plays whose characters remain unaffected by the foreshadowing, since in many of these cases it appears to be a device used mainly for the benefit of the spectators, and rarely has any bearing on the action itself. Such a device could be used, for example, at the end of the play to warn the audience that the protagonist is about to meet his death, an event that is fulfilled so quickly after the warning that the foreshadowing does nothing more than heighten the dramatic suspense of the moment. Lope was not averse to using these devices merely for the purpose of entertaining the public, for he knew that the slightest boredom in the pit could be fatal, but we will be concerned now mainly with the performances in which the technique of foreshadowing affects the entire structure of the work, contributing to the tragic aspects of the characters and to the dramatic irony of the whole play.

The subject of foreshadowing necessarily leads to the complicated problems inherent in both tragedy and irony—concepts which are, of course, too broad to be dealt with here at any length. It should be made clear, however, that the *quality* of self-awareness acquired by the characters through the various devices of foreshadowing provides an essential key to understanding Lope's use of irony and tragedy. It has been pointed out that the characters insist on turning a deaf ear to the voice of fate, preferring instead to deceive themselves about the meaning of the warnings they receive. The audience, on the other hand, observes their actions with a certain disinterested detachment, and therefore is able to understand the warnings for what they are, as well as see through the self-deception of the characters. The audience is better able to distinguish between the appearance and the reality of the character's situation, so he becomes an ironic figure whose frequently self-imposed ignorance of his fate is quite obvious to the spectators. But self-awareness cannot always be successfully blanketed with deception and rationalizations, and so the character almost invariably is troubled by inner conflicts resulting from the clash between his foreknowledge and his desire not to know. To the extent that he knows less than the audience, then, he is an ironic figure. But to the extent that he is aware of what is in store for him yet is unable or unwilling to do anything about it, he is a tragic figure whose inevitable destiny arouses pity and fear in the spectators.

Some definitions of irony

Connop Thirlwall is the first modern critic to discuss what is now generally referred to as "dramatic irony."[2] He divides his definition of irony into four categories, three of which are useful in establishing a basis for studying Lope's use of irony and ironic devices.[3]

1. *Verbal irony:* This type of irony highlights the contrast between thought and expression, and is usually either sarcastic or polemical. In Golden Age plays verbal irony is most often found in the speeches of the *graciosos*, whose cynical views are in humorous contrast to the idealism of their masters or mistresses. Thus Tello, after listening to Alonso's impassioned speech about his love for Inés, mutters *"Sólo te falta decir:/ 'un poco te quiero,' Inés."* (*"The only thing you haven't said to her yet is 'I love you just a tiny bit, Inés'."* (*El Caballero de Olmedo*, II, i)

2. *Practical irony:* Now more commonly known as the "irony of events" (to distinguish it more clearly from the irony which may be found in words or in speech), this kind of irony draws a painful contrast between hopes and their realization, which the audience often sees as "the mockery of fate." Thirlwall distinguishes two kinds of practical irony:

   a) *Malignant* or *wanton irony:* A character humors the folly of somebody else by means of "flattery which, under the mask of friendship, deliberately

---

[2] Bishop Connop Thirlwall, "On the Irony of Sophocles," The Philological Museum, II (1833), 483-527.
[3] I shall leave out the category that Thirlwall calls "dialectic irony" (now generally referred to as "Socratic irony"), since intellectual dialogues of this kind are not found in the plays to be dealt with in this book.

cherishes passions and panders to wishes which are hurrying their unconscious slave to ruin" (p. 485). Fabia is the obvious example of such an individual. A case in point is her implied use of the exhortation, "Collige, Virgo, rosās" ("Gather ye rosebuds while ye may") in order to convince Inés to surrender to Don Alonso (*El caballero de Olmedo,* I, v).

b) *Benevolent:* An intelligent character of superior understanding finds it necessary to assent to the folly of another, knowing that it is futile to reason with one who has already surrendered to passion. Benevolent irony is usually found in the confidantes, or in any other sympathetic character who recognizes his friend's difficult dilemma. Leonor is a good example of this, for she knows from the start that Inés's love is dangerous, and yet she can do nothing at all to dissuade her (*El caballero de Olmedo).*

3. *The irony of divided sympathy:* This is the kind of irony that is experienced by a spectator who views (from a superior and detached position) the argument between two contenders who are each partly right and partly wrong, and who knows that neither of them can possibly understand the deeper truth to be found in their combined argument. Thirlwall gives us as an example the case of Antigone and Creon. In Lope's theatre, however, the contenders are not so evenly matched from a moral or philosophical point of view, although Rodolfo and Otón come quite close (*La imperial de Otón*). Lope's characters are often better suited to an elaboration of this ironic device, known as "irony as emotional dissonance," to be discussed later.

It is important to note, then, that in all the cases that are mentioned by Thirlwall, irony emerges as a result of the contrast between an ignorant character and another individual whose superior knowledge allows him to see the folly of the former's hopes and expectations. This is the crux of the matter—all the other definitions will in one way or another concern themselves primarily with variations on the theme of the contrast between appearance and reality.

J.A.K. Thomson supplies a good label for the detached and superior character (or spectator) by reminding us that the word *eirōn* was applied by the Greeks to certain characters who, like Socrates, could see through the ignorant pose of an *alazōn* and deftly expose him by the use of ironic argument[4]. These terms were used only for figures in comedies, but for the sake of convenience *eirōn* has been expanded to include all those who see more deeply than the ironic dupe, whether they be spectators, other characters, or the playwright.

After a careful examination of the different uses of irony in comedy and tragedy, Thomson offers a definition for what has been called *Sophoclean irony:*[5] "It is a device, often strikingly effective, which puts in the mouth of a character language whose full significance is not perceived by himself but only by his hearers, who know, as he does not, the doom that awaits him" (p.35). An excellent example of Sophoclean irony can be found in Act I, i of *El caballero de Olmedo,* when Don Alonso describes his first meeting with Inés:

---

[4] *Irony, an Historical Introduction,* Cambridge (Harvard University Press), 1927. "*Alazoneia* in Comedy is another aspect of what in Tragedy is called *hubris*... The essence of both is 'going too far'... What is funny in the imposter is tragic in the heroic man" (p. 35).

[5] This term was coined in the nineteenth century, and has been referred to as "tragic irony" or "dramatic irony". In addition to the essays mentioned in this section, see María Rosa Lida de Malkiel, *Introducción al teatro de Sófocles,* undated lecture in *Essays and Addresses,* Cambridge (1907), pp. 29-33.

En una capilla entraron;
yo, que siguiéndolas iba,
entré imaginando bodas.
¡Tanto quien ama imagina!
Vime sentenciado a muerte,
porque el amor me decía:
"Mañana mueres, pues hoy
te meten en la capilla."

("[The maidens] entered a chapel and I followed them inside, imagining wedding bells. That is how foolish a lover can be! I saw myself sentenced to death, because love said to me: *Tomorrow you die, for today they put you in the chapel.*")

The audience knows the ballad and foresees Don Alonso's fate, but Alonso himself is not yet consciously aware of what is in store for him. Thomson goes on to discuss the dramatic effect of the spectators' foreknowledge, which directs their attention away from the question *What will happen?* (a suspense device used mainly in mysteries and melodramas) and invites them to contemplate instead the questions *How, why, and when will it happen?* Without foreknowledge, of course, there would be no irony, and without irony the dramatic impact of a play would be considerably decreased.

Sedgewick expands Thomson's definition of Sophoclean irony to include not only the ironic figure's language and situation, but also a speculation of his own concerning the character's reaction if he could be made aware of his own deception: "the situation as it *seems* to him differs from the situation as it *is:* he is ignorant that appearance is being contradicted by reality; he would act differently if he knew."[6] The last phrase of Sedgewick's definition is certainly applicable to most plays, both tragic and comic, but in some cases

---

[6] G.G. Sedgewick, *Of Irony, Especially in Drama* (1935), Toronto (Univ. of Toronto Press) 1967, p. 49.

one has to doubt that the ironic figure would act differently even if he were to know. This is particularly true of *El Caballero de Olmedo,* so this question will be examined in greater detail later in the section where the play is discussed. A.R. Thompson usually follows the definitions outlined above, but he adds a term which is of special interest to this study when he speaks of "irony as emotional dissonance."[7] This involves the conflict of reason and passion within the ironic character himself, which allows the audience to view his struggle with detached sympathy and concern (in the case of tragedy), or with amusement (in the case of comedy). This is similar to Thirlwall's irony of divided sympathy in that the spectator is aware that there is something both noble and destructive about the amorous passion felt by the hero (the inner contenders are partly right and partly wrong).[8] It differs from the irony of divided sympathy in that the contenders are not represented by two evenly matched forces *within* the protagonist. Irony as emotional dissonance is found mostly in Lope's tragedies that deal with the conflict between passion and reason, as we shall see when we examine the three best examples of the irony and tragedy of passionate love: *La desdichada Estefanía* ("The Sorrowful Stephanie"), *La imperial de Otón,* and *El caballero de Olmedo.*

These opinions are by no means the only ones offered by the above-mentioned scholars, who represent only a small part of what has been published on the subject of dramatic

---

[7] A.R. Thompson, *The Dry Mock,* Berkeley, 1948, p. 131

[8] This was not true of the Greek spectator, who viewed amorous passion as being a punishment from the gods. As for the Golden Age spectator, his sympathy was generally not extended to those characters whose passion was directed at unwilling love objects; those who attempted to rape women were punished, and those who tried to force others to love them were held up to ridicule. For a Golden Age audience the sin of amorous passion was not lust in and of itself, but the pride and self-interest that sometimes attended it.

irony,[9] but the definitions that have just been discussed are particularly pertinent to the kind of irony that Lope used in his plays. We shall find many examples of verbal irony, practical irony, and irony as emotional dissonance in the following pages as we contemplate, along with the audience, the tragic struggle of the characters to bring into harmony the conflicting demands of their conscience as well as their circumstances.

Characteristics of Lope's tragic figures

For the sake of brevity and convenience, let it be understood that the idea of tragedy as it appears in this thesis is based on Aristotle's original description in the *Poetics,* which will be used as a standard of measurement of Lope's theatrical practices. Lope's own ideas of what constituted a tragedy were based mainly on the theories of neo-Aristotelian commentators,[10] which led him to apply the term to any serious drama where the characters were noble, the actions lofty, the subject matter "historic" (to be understood in its broadest context), the style elevated, or the protagonist met with death.[11]

---

[9] In addition to the works cited in the text and footnotes of the preceding pages, the following books are also very illuminating: María Rosa Lida de Malkiel, *La originalidad artística de "La Celestina",* Buenos Aires, 1962, chap. IX ("La ironía"), pp. 250-257; Donald E. Soule, *Irony in the Drama, an Essay on Impersonation, Shock, and Catharsis,* Chapel Hill (University of North Carolina Press) 1959; and Norman Knox, *The Word Irony and its Context, 1500-1755,* Durham, (Duke Univ. Press) 1961.

[10] Pérez y Escribano (*Afirmaciones de Lope de Vega sobre preceptiva dramática)* feels that Lope's knowledge of Aristotle came mainly from his reading of Castelvetro (p.87). By the time he read El Pinciano, his ideas on dramatic theory were already well established.

[11] Edwin Morby, "Some observations on *tragedia* and *tragicomedia* in Lope," HR, XI, 1943. On pp. 191-192 he lists Spingarn's distinctions

But as many critics have pointed out, "la tragedia al estilo español" was not always a tragedy in a strictly Aristotelian sense,[12] and Lope's was certainly no exception. Some of the reasons for his failure to produce "pure" tragedies have been discussed by Rennert and Castro, who observed that he was usually very reluctant to end his plays on a sad note,[13] an observation that is corroborated by many examples in this thesis, such as *El marido más firme* and *El robo de Dina* ("The Most Steadfast Husband" and "The Abduction of Dinah"). Morby mentions that Lope often chose to continue "the play for some distance beyond what might have been the tragic dénouement" (p. 208), as in the case of *El bastardo Mudarra* and *El último godo* ("The Last Goth"). Another important point was made by MacCurdy when he wrote that the figures of the Spanish Golden Age drama were usually "stock characters" that tended to be either all "good" or all "bad", either innocent victims or downright villains.[14]

This leads to melodrama and not to tragedy, as will be evident in various plays to be analyzed below, such as *La inocente sangre* ("Innocent Blood") and *El marqués de Mantua*. According to the Aristotelian definition, the tragic hero should ideally be a noble figure with a tragic flaw, who must be partially responsible for the fate that is caused by his *hamartia* (which could be interpreted as either a moral weak-

---

between tragedy and comedy as they were understood from the post-classical era to the Renaissance.

[12] "En España no hubo tragedia, ni en los tiempos del Renacimiento," from F. Sáinz de Robles, *Ensayo de un diccionario de la literatura,* Madrid, 1949, I, 1273. This opinion was particularly prevalent among the German Romantic scholars; Morby quotes Schack as saying that Lope's distinctions between tragedy and comedy were "capricious and unimportant". *Art. cit.,* p. 186.

[13] *Vida de Lope de Vega,* quoted by Morby, *art. cit.,* p. 207.

[14] Raymond R. MacCurdy, *Francisco de Rojas Zorrilla and the Tragedy,* Albuquerque, 1958, p. 37.

ness or an intellectual blindness). At the same time he should to some extent be aware of his impending doom, even if he does not fully understand it until the moment of *anagnōrisis* (recognition). His *hamartia* (tragic flaw), then, causes him to initiate an action whose results will inevitably be detrimental to his happiness or well-being, while at the same time his insight (inspired by the information provided by the devices of foreshadowing) warns him of the underlying folly of his action. Thus he must struggle with the conflicting demands of reason and desire, but we know, and to some extent he knows, too, that his struggle is doomed from the start. The spectators see more clearly than he does the exact nature of his fate, so they not only appreciate the irony inherent in his false expectations, but they are also moved by the fact that he is tragically unable to do anything to change his destiny.

In short, if the character were to be completely self-aware there would be no irony, and if the character were totally unaware there would be no tragedy. There must be a balance between ignorance and awareness in order to produce tragic irony, and in Lope's theatre this balance occurs most often in those tragedies that deal with amorous passion. The balance is interrupted at the point when the hero is no longer ignorant or semi-aware, that is to say, at the moment of recognition (*anagnōrisis*). At that time there is a reversal from a state of innocence to a state of knowledge and insight, and the protagonist, at this moment of self-recognition, gets a brief glimpse of the underlying truth of his condition. He sees beyond the immediate problem of his passion, and perceives, finally, both the nobility and the total absurdity of human strivings.

This is dramatized with particular skill in *La imperial de Otón,* when the King finally understands the deeper meaning of everything that he has been trying to accomplish. Lope's characters are quite often brought to their moment of recognition as a result of another, graphically symbolic form of self-confrontation with the silent *sombra.* This silent shadow is sometimes seen by the hero as a representation of himself, a sort of extension of his own being, and the experience fills him with a feeling of dread inspired by his self-knowledge and loss of innocence. At this point he begins to lose his character as an ironic dupe, and acquires the tragic dimensions of the hero who knows, but cannot accept or even admit his knowledge. The dilemma of his passion has acted as a catalyst for his dramatic recognition.

Edwin Morby has an acute understanding of the tragic dimensions of the passionate lovers in Lope's serious plays (as opposed to the more frivolous, conventional lovers of the light comedies) when he writes that "the position of love as a source of tragic conflict in Lope invites serious study; though it must be recognized that the ratio of love tragedies is much higher in comparison with the practice of antiquity than with that of Lope's contemporaries, even in orthodox circles. In bringing love to the fore, Lope is only following a tendency that was noticeable throughout the Renaissance."[15]

That tendency not only "brings love to the fore," but it treats passion in a manner that is very different from the way the classical writers treated it. C.S. Lewis reminds us that "in ancient literature love seldom rises above the levels of merry sensuality or domestic comfort, except to be treated as a tragic madness... which plunges otherwise sane people... into crime and disgrace."[16]

In the Golden Age theatre love as "merry sensuality" is generally reserved for the *graciosos* (comic characters) and other figures of lowly rank; only noblemen are capable of feeling passion as a "tragic madness," but far from being considered disgraceful or criminal, these passionate lovers elicited the full sympathy of the audience, who saw them as noble characters whose only flaw was that they loved not

---

[15] Edwin Morby, art. cit., p. 199.
[16] *The Allegory of Love,* New York, 1958, p. 4.

wisely but too well. This attitude, which differs so much from that of the ancients, can be traced back to the eleventh century when passion began to be considered an ennobling force, productive of all virtue and all good. This is the point of view of Capellanus in his first two books,[17] and it is echoed by writings coming from a large variety of sources, both European and Eastern (i.e. Arabic and Semitic).

It is not our concern here to document the sources of the literature of love in the Golden Age;[18] suffice it to say that the passionate hero fulfilled the Aristotelian description of "character" in that he was neither villainous nor perfect, but a noble creature that became the inevitable victim of his own blindness.

Passion may well be an ennobling force, but there was a parallel current of opinion which saw it as a destructive force as well, as even Capellanus himself was to maintain in his third book, a sort of *reprobatio amoris* that is reminiscent of so many others written throughout the ages: "For another reason I urge you not to love: that is because in a wise man wisdom loses its function if he loves. No matter how full of wisdom any man may be, if he is seduced to the work of Venus he cannot be moderate or restrain by his wisdom the impulse of wantonness or keep from doing the things that lead to death."[19] This is the tragedy of the passionate lover,

---

[17] Andreas Capellanus, *The Art of Courtly Love,* trans. John J. Parry, New York, 1957.

[18] For an excellent bibliography on the subject, see Otis H. Green, *Spain and the Western Tradition,* 4 vols., Madison (University of Wisconsin Press), 1968; and Erna Ruth Berndt, *Amor, muerte, y fortuna en "La Celestina",* Madrid, 1963. These books concentrate on European sources; for Arabic and Semitic influences, see Américo Castro, *La realidad histórica de España,* Mexico, 1954; and A.J. Denomy, *The Heresy of Courtly Love,* New York, 1947.

[19] *The Art of Courtly Love,* p. 48. Here "love" refers to what I have been calling "passion," which is based on the urges of *erōs* as opposed to those of *agapē*.

caught as he is between the demands of "wisdom" and the "impulse of wantonness" that eventually causes him to become the worker of his own downfall.

F. L. Lucas makes the point clearly: "It is the perpetual tragic irony of the Tragedy of Life that again and again men laboriously contrive their own annihilation, or kill the thing they love, for the most poignant tragedy of human existence is the work of human blindness... The Tragedy of Errors.

"In tragic life, God wot,
no villain need be. Passions spin the plot:
we are betrayed by what is false within."[20]

Criteria for selecting plays

The primary purpose of this book is to explore the feelings and reactions of the characters, who by means of the devices of foreshadowing (astrologers, ghosts, omens, and dreams) come to share with the audience and the reader a certain awareness of what lies ahead. In order to concentrate on the ironic and tragic dimensions of the protagonists, I generally read only those plays that could be described as "serious" or perhaps "tragic" in the Aristotelian sense. For this purpose I found Diego Marín's book helpful, since it gives a plot outline of Lope's tragedies and tragicomedies.[21] Edwin Morby's article was also helpful in this respect, for he mentions a good number of serious plays and their reasons for qualifying as tragedies (both in the neo-Aristotelian and

---

[20] Lucas, *Tragedy*, New York, 1957, pp. 97-98, quoting George Meredith, "Love's Grave."

[21] Diego Marín, *La intriga secundaria en el teatro de Lope de Vega*, Mexico, 1958.

the modern sense of the word).[22] Of equal value is the information that is given in the preliminary discussions to the Academy and New Academy editions of Lope's plays written by Menéndez y Pelayo and Cotarelo y Mori, respectively.[23] Montesinos mentions various plays where *sombras* appear,[24] Nagy analyzes a dozen plays containing certain themes from *La Celestina*[25] ("The Go-Between"), and Halstead analyzes plays that deal with free will.[26]

On the basis of the information gathered from these sources and numerous others, I proceeded to read a selection of seventy plays, out of which I chose thirty-six to be discussed in this volume. It goes without saying that foreshadowing inevitably occurs in Lope's epic, ballad, biblical, historical, and mythological plays, for both the reader and the audience are bound to be familiar with the well-known plot material. Since I was primarily concerned with the *protagonist's* reaction to his own foreknowledge, however, I limited my choice of plays to those in which it was evident that the devices of foreshadowing were heard and understood not only by the audience but by the protagonist himself. It soon became clear that his foreknowledge did not always make him a potentially tragic figure, struggling to overcome an inevitable fate which he himself foresaw. Sometimes Lope's use of dreams, omens, ghosts, and prophecies tended

[22] Edwin S. Morby, "Some observations on *Tragedia* and *Tragicomedia* in Lope," *HR,* XI (1943), pp. 185-209.
[23] *Obras de Lope de Vega,* publicadas por la Real Academia Española, ed. M. Menéndez y Pelayo, Madrid, 1890-1913 (15 vols.). *Obras de Lope de Vega,* publicadas por la Real Academia Española (Nueva Edición), ed. Emilio Cotarelo y Mori, Madrid, 1916-1930 (13 vols.).
[24] *El marqués de Las Navas,* ed. J.F. Montesinos, *TAE,* VI, Madrid, 1925.
[25] Edward Nagy, *Lope de Vega y la Celestina: Perspectiva pseudo-celestinesca en comedias de Lope* (Cuadernos de la Facultad de Filosofía, Letras, y Ciencias, 39), Mexico (Univ. Veracruzana), 1968.
[26] Frank G. Halstead, "The Attitude of Lope de Vega toward Astrology and Astronomy," *HR,* VII (1939), 205-219.

only to amuse, frighten, or appeal to a generally superstitious audience, or they were used merely to heighten the dramatic intensity of a particular scene. It became clear that certain protagonists had a peculiar self-awareness *without* needing to be warned by specific devices of foreshadowing, as in the cases of *El niño inocente de la Guardia* ("The Innocent Boy of La Guardia), *Porfiar hasta morir* ("The Struggle unto Death") and *Lo fingido verdadero* ("When Pretense Turns Out To Be True").

At this point the thesis could have gone in either of two directions: I could have concentrated entirely on the problem of self-awareness and foreknowledge on the part of the protagonists and the resulting tragic and ironic character of their destinies, or I could have emphasized Lope's use of the devices of foreshadowing and their effect on the play as a whole, as well as their effect on the consciousness of the protagonist. I finally chose the latter approach because it offered a broader basis on which to analyze Lope's plays, and it also allowed me to examine certain qualities that are typical of Lope and his theatre: his puckish delight in playing with the audience's credulity, his sense of dramatic exigency in introducing supernatural phenomena, his facile recourse to these same phenomena when the tempo was beginning to slow down, his appealing way of taking the audience into his confidence when it came to questions of semi-taboo superstitions and dark mysteries that interested everyone but were spoken of only with great caution in public.

In conclusion, then, the criteria used for selecting the plays depended almost exclusively on specific devices of foreshadowing such as ghosts, omens, dreams, predictions, prophecies, and kledonomancy, all of which were understood or heard by the protagonist. Their effect on him and his reaction to them will be of prime concern in the analyses that follow.

Structure of this thesis

In general, the thesis progresses from a trivial use of the
devices of foreshadowing to their most meaningful use, and
this holds true for each individual section as well as for the
thesis itself. Hence, the first section of Part One is devoted to
Lope's use of vocal *sombras* which, as it turns out, were less
effective and less dramatic than the silent *sombras* that will
be studied later. In the same way, this section progresses
from a study of the non-predictive vocal *sombras* whose
function is entirely prosaic, to the predictive vocal *sombras*
who at least warn the protagonists of what is to come. The
sections on omens, dreams, kledonomancy, and prophecies
are structured in the same way.

In Part Two there are three plays in which Lope attempts
to explore the philosophical aspects of foreknowledge and
self-awareness, which lead him to examine the questions of
free will and determinism. Although he does not delve as
deeply as Tirso de Molina or Calderón de la Barca into the
complex problems that are raised by these particular issues,
he is concerned with the questions of human destiny and the
extent to which we can or cannot control it.

Part Three offers a selection of plays that deal with the
question of amorous passion and the conflicts that are necessarily felt by the protagonists who, warned by the devices of
foreshadowing, foresee but cannot avoid their tragic destinies. Some of the questions in this chapter evolve quite
naturally from the material in Part Two, for it becomes evident that the one force that can most successfully overcome
man's free will is amorous passion. Those doomed lovers
who were aware of the danger and yet knew themselves to be
powerless to avoid it turned out to be tragic figures, tragic
because they were responsible for their fate, yet victimized
by their own passion. They were also ironic figures to the
spectators, who contemplated their false hopes and self-
deception from a distance which allowed them the necessary

objectivity to see reality as it was, and not as the protagonists hoped it would be. It is a curious fact that every one of the silent *sombras* I know of in Lope's theatre appears before a passionate lover who is undergoing just the kind of tragic conflict outlined here.

I shall attempt to analyze as carefully as possible Lope's use of these intriguing silent *sombras,* which to my mind are the most successful and meaningful of all his devices of foreshadowing. This section ends with an analysis of *El caballero de Olmedo,* one of Lope's greatest plays and the one which best illustrates the ideas and theories set forth in the final chapter.

PART ONE

The Devices of Foreshadowing

VOCAL "SOMBRAS" ("GHOSTS")

O f the many technical devices used by Lope de Vega to achieve a dramatic effect, the vocal and silent *sombras* seem to have appealed to him more than any other, judging by their frequent appearance throughout the entire corpus of his plays. In this section we shall be dealing only with the vocal variety, and it will soon become evident that Menéndez y Pelayo must have overlooked these talkative ghosts when he wrote *"En Lope lo sobrenatural es siempre muy rápido, y cruza por la escena como un relámpago."*[27] ("In Lope supernatural phenomena always move rapidly, crossing the stage as if they were lightning bolts.")

The vocal *sombras* were of two kinds: those that came to settle their own unfinished business on earth or reward the living for their charity, and those that came to predict the future of the protagonist. Certainly the function of the first group was far less interesting than that of the second; their purpose was generally quite prosaic, or at best amusing. The function of the predictive vocal *sombras,* however, produced the kind of ironic effect which has already been discussed in the introduction, for the audience, forewarned by the *sombra,* was able to see and know both the appearance and the reality

---

[27] *Obras de Lope de Vega,* publicadas por la Real Academia Española, ed. M. Menéndez y Pelayo, Madrid, 1890-1913, vol. VI, p. xcii. This edition will hereinafter be referred to simply as *"Acad."*

of the protagonist's situation. But the ghost's warnings were never entirely lost on the protagonist, for he, too, was able to see the future as it was described in the prediction, and yet despite his foreknowledge he was often unwilling to avoid or modify the inevitable pattern of his destiny.

In this section we shall see that those characters who refused to avoid danger (in spite of the urgent warnings of the vocal sombras) did so because they consciously wished to make the ultimate sacrifice for their honor or for the sake of their country. They died a heroic death, a death that was inevitable only because the protagonist's virtue and courage did not permit him to accept a less noble alternative. Unlike the passionate lovers discussed in Part Three, these characters felt very little inner conflict as a result of their foreknowledge of death, for they sensed that their fate was in harmony with their highest ideals.

The lovers in Part Three, on the other hand, found themselves struggling with numerous paradoxes having to do with the nature of passion itself, so they eventually succumbed to their fate in spite of their better judgment and in spite of the silent *sombras* who tried in vain to deter them. In contrast to the heroic characters that will be studied in this section, the lovers of Part Three are largely tragic figures whose flaws made it impossible for them to exercise any freedom of choice. The function and meaning of the silent *sombras* will be examined at length in the appropriate sections; meanwhile we shall start out by discussing the non-predictive vocal *sombras,* and from there we shall go on to study the function of the predictive vocal ones.

Even the most cursory examination of the role of the nonpredictive vocal *sombras* makes it obvious that they are used mainly for the purpose of entertainment, for they add little or nothing to the dramatic tension of the play. Montesinos, after noting the dramatic efficacy of the silent specters, points out that the longer the vocal ones remain on the stage to chat, the less effect they have on the characters and on the audience.[28]

El Marqués de Las Navas
("The Marquis of Las Navas")

This is particularly true of *El Marqués de Las Navas,* in which the overly loquacious *sombra* takes up an inordinate amount of time telling the *Marqués* (who had killed him in an honorable sword fight toward the end of the second act) all about his debts which had to be paid before he could get out of purgatory. He also asks his murderer to have some masses said for him so that his purgatorial visit might be shortened, a request that is dutifully fulfilled. Although there is no foreshadowing to speak of in this play, the amiable and unrancorous attitude of the murdered man is of interest as an illustration of the Catholic position on the subject of death, a matter that is taken seriously but with no note of ultimate despair. The death of the body is of small consequence; it is one's destiny after life on earth that is of supreme concern.

El príncipe perfecto
("The Perfect Prince")

Another example of a similar situation appears in *El príncipe perfecto* (The Perfect Prince), part I, when the ghost of a certain *pícaro* (a scoundrel whom the Prince had killed) reappears to ask him to have masses said for his soul. He embarks on the rather prosaic problem of money when he requests that the King (formerly the Prince) do him the favor of giving his *novia* (fiancée) a dowry so that she might find a suitable husband. The altruism of this soul is noteworthy, for

---

[28] *El marqués de las Navas,* introduction and notes by J. F. Montesinos, TAE, VI, 168-169.

now that he is free from worldly shortcomings such as pride and jealousy, he acquires Christian virtue at last. Unlike the lovers in the plays to be analyzed in Part Three, the King is undaunted by the apparition of the ghost:

> *¿Eres cuerpo vano*
> *o fantástica ilusión?*
> *¿O eres sombra de mi mismo,*
> *que con esta luz se causa?*
> *Entra, pues, dime la causa;*
> *que aunque del obscuro abismo*
> *vengas, no has de hallar temor*
> *en este pecho. ¿Quién eres?*[29]

("Are you an apparition or some figment of my imagination, or are you my own shadow that I spy in this light? Come in, then, and tell me what you want; for even if you are from the dark underworld, you shall not find any fear in this breast of mine. Who are you?")

The ghost identifies himself and asks the King to follow him. The King is ready to do so, showing no fear at all:

> *Parte delante;*
> *que con la espada en la mano*
> *y las armas de Cristiano,*
> *no hay ilusión que me espante.*
>
> (*Acad.* X, 477b)

("Lead the way, for with my trusty sword in my hand and my Christian armor on my back, I have no fear of apparitions.")

---

[29] *Acad.* X, 477a. I have copied the texts as they appear in this edition, without modernizing the spelling or accents.

Passionate lovers in Lope's theatre were always terrifed of specters because, as we shall see, they were all aware that they were themselves courting danger and death. The King's conscience in this play, however, is absolutely clear, for he has been consistently portrayed as a virtuous Prince (with the exception of the first scenes in which he engaged in a few so-called peccadillos, one of which was the murder of the *pícaro* or "rogue" which occurred while he was defending the honor of his friend). To the guiltless and honorable man it is not the spiritual but rather the human apparitions that are worrisome. Thus the King complains to the Prior because he finds he is the object of Doña Clara's passionate desire:

> *Toda esta noche, Prior,*
> *me buscan muertos y vivos.*
> *No son de temer los muertos;*
> *los vivos son de temer,*
> *y deseos de mujer*
> *son vivos peligros ciertos.*
> *Los muertos piden, Prior,*
> *misas y satisfacciones,*
> *y las vivas ocasiones*
> *donde se pierde el honor.*
>
> (*Acad. X,* 479b)

("All night long, Prior, I've been sought by both the living and the dead. Yet it's not the dead who should be feared, but the living... and a woman's desire should be feared most of all. The dead, Prior, ask for masses and revenge, but the living ask for favors that cause men to lose their honor.")

When a woman's love is seen to threaten a man's honor, we are reminded of the third book of Andreas Capellanus' *De reprobatione amoris* ("*On the Iniquity of Erotic Desire*") as well as the anti-feminist literature popular throughout the

Middle Ages.[30] But Lope tempers the King's attitude with a sensitive, tolerant view of Doña Clara's amorous desire—he never treats her harshly or thinks of her as a "wicked temptress," nor does he find it necessary to sever all relations with her, for he promises to visit her in the convent to which she finally decides to retire.

Apart from the humor, the play serves as an excellent commentary on the nature of *agapē* and *erōs* as it juxtaposes the Christian morality of the King with the erotic passion of Don Juan. The latter has spurned the doting Leonor (whose love has begun to irritate him) for the disdainful Doña Clara, a *belle dame sans merci* if there ever was one. We find most of the elements of erotic passion in a clear-sighted sonnet spoken by Don Juan:

> *Aborrecí querido, y olvidado*
> *quiero por condición de amor injusto;*
> *que la satisfacción causa disgusto,*
> *y la sospecha enciende un pecho helado.*
>
> *A quien me quiere olvido, y, desamado,*
> *adorar un desdén tengo por justo:*
> *tal es la diferencia con que el gusto*
> *desprecia amado, y quiere despreciado.*
>
> *Amor que los deseos satisface,*
> *ya no es amor, sino amoroso empleo,*
> *que quiere aquello que su gusto hace.*
>
> *Pues por tan claras experiencias veo*
> *que en la dificultad el amor nace,*
> *y en la facilidad muere el deseo.*
>
> (*Acad. X,* 479b)

---

[30] Cf. Alfonso Martínez de Toledo, *El arcipreste de Talavera* (better known as *El Corbacho*), especially the introduction and notes by Mario Penna, Turin, n.d.

("When I was loved I was disdainful, but now that I am for-gotten I love again because love is unfair; for satisfaction causes disappointment, but suspicion ignites a frozen heart. I ignore the one who loves me, but when I am jilted I revel in the disdain: pleasure is perverse, for it scorns love and loves contempt. When love satisfies desire, it ceases to be love and becomes mere love-play, which wants whatever provides pleasure. So as a result of these clear experiences I see that love is born when it encounters difficulties, but desire dies when things are easy.")

But Don Juan's passion is not of the doomed variety, for he plays the game as a means to an end (that of enjoying the excitement and fulfillment of sexual desire) and not as an end in itself, so he does not die. Instead, he resigns himself rather good-naturedly to marrying Doña Leonor, to whom he had been previously engaged.

The absence of foreshadowing in this entertaining play is appropriate to its generally light-hearted spirit. The ghost comes not to warn but to express a *queja* (complaint) born of his desire to do what is right by the woman he once loved.

Don Juan de Castro (Parts I and II)

Don Juan de Castro offers yet another example of a ghost who comes not to warn but rather, in this case, to reward the protagonist for giving him a decent Christian burial, paying for his masses, and taking care of his debts so that he might not die excommunicated. This he does by causing the hero to win a joust, and consequently a kingdom, riches, and the hand of his lady. Although the appreciative ghost clearly states his intentions at the beginning of the play, the audience is kept amused throughout the six acts by the disguises, adventures, separations, imprisonments and other dramatic coups that Lope dreams up. The ghost is an ingenuous sort of creature this time, playing a role halfway between puppeteer and fairy godmother.

El premio de la hermosura
("Beauty's Reward")

Sometimes ghosts can be a source of comfort and help. In the first act of *El premio de la hermosura*, Cardiloro is contemplating suicide because his lady, promised to another, has died of a broken heart. Just as he is about to commit the fatal act, however, the ghost of his father appears and diverts him from his despair by giving him some sound advice. Then a magician sends him into a magic sleep of forgetfulness, a forgetfulness that apparently had its effect on the author as well, for Cardiloro (who seemed to be the protagonist) never reappears for the rest of the play. This would not be unusual in a pastoral novel, but the dramatic unity of a stage production is ordinarily jeopardized by the disappearance of the central character. Although neither Lope nor his audience put undue emphasis on unity, it could be argued that the third act tends to rescue the first from its apparent irrelevancy by once again introducing the question of suicide or "death by a broken heart": Tisbe hears a voice that predicts that she will see her lover die, after which she will then die herself. The prediction is quickly fulfilled, offering us a rare example of suicide in Lope's theatre.[31]

El ganso de oro
("The Golden Goose")

Although Lope de Vega's most effective predictive *sombras* are messengers of doom, *El ganso de oro* offers an example

---

[31] Although the cause of Tisbe's death was not clearly stated in the play, Lope specifically says it was suicide in his *relación* (Acad. XIII). Despite the foreshadowing, I cannot say there is much irony in this play, which was devised mainly to entertain the audience in the manner of a pastoral novel (whose characters it imitates) or a Byzantine novel (whose structure it attempts, with difficulty, to dramatize).

of a ghost who brings welcome news: the hero will redeem Naples and save it from the plague. But far from putting the audience at rest as far as foreseeing the outcome is concerned the news only serves to perplex us, for if the humble shepherd goes to Naples and becomes a hero, how will this affect the life and love of the shepherdess who is waiting in Arcadia for his return? If he is raised from a lowly station to a high one, will the two be able to marry? Despite the prediction of the *sombra,* the outcome is hidden from us until the end, when it suddenly turns out (in true Lope style) that the shepherdess is the daughter of a great magician, which therefore makes her worthy of marrying the shepherd, even though he has since become the King of Naples.

El Arauco domado
("The Araucan Tamed")

El Arauco domado provides a good example of what has already been said at the beginning of this section about the function of predictive vocal *sombras.* Lope treats the protagonist, Caupolicán, in much the same way as Ercilla did, investing him and his counselors with honor and courage. Despite the warnings of the devil Pillán, who predicted that the Spanish would end up conquering the Indians and founding many cities, Caupolicán nevertheless rallies his soldiers and inspires them with the desire to protect their freedom and their country. Although he is at first firmly resolved not to consider the possibility of surrender, his decision begins to waver toward the end of the second act after he has lost a skirmish, and after his wife has complained of having seen a series of bad omens (*Acad.* XII, 623a). In his moment of hesitation a tree opens before him and a *sombra* appears; he warns Caupolicán that the Spaniards are making progress in their conquest for they have already founded a city in the country, but although he knows the superior strength of the enemy, the *sombra* encourages the Inca to fight them in spite of everything, reminding him that it is better to die with honor than to live on one's knees. Caupolicán attacks the Spaniards with renewed ardor—despite his foreknowledge of his predestined defeat—fighting bravely until he is finally captured. He reacts with heroism and dignity to the fate he knew awaited him:

> *Libre nací,*
> *la libertad defendí*
> *de mi patria y de mi ley;*
> *la vuestra no la he tomado.*
>
> (*Acad.* XII, 633b)

("I was born free, I defended the freedom of my country and my law; I did not take yours.")

The Spaniards tie Caupolicán to a stake, and shortly thereafter he converts to Catholicism and dies a martyr. His worldly defeat has ironically become a spiritual victory.

El duque de Viseo
("The Duke of Viseo")

The first two acts of *El duque de Viseo* are devoted to esta-blishing the dramatic necessity of the Duke's eventual death: the cold and inhuman character of the King,[32] envy among the courtiers, affronted honor, the desire for revenge, self-interest and perfidy—all prepare the audience for the inevi-table outcome. This makes the mysterious voices and the portents of the third act all the more effective in that they redouble the forebodings of the characters and the spectators. The ghost of Guimarans (who had been treacherously mur-dered by the King) appears for the purpose of warning the

---

[32] The perverse King here is not Spanish, but Portuguese. This fulfills the patriotic expectations of both Lope and his audience.

Duke to be wary of the King, but he is a true and faithful vassal and refuses to take any action against the monarch. His innocence and scrupulous loyalty make him a sympathetic figure, but his foreknowledge of his destiny and his conscious refusal to avoid it by compromising his values as a nobleman give him a truly heroic dimension.

Contra valor no hay desdicha
("No Misfortune Shall Prevail Against Bravery")

Although the *sombras* in the last three plays predicted the future and warned the characters of approaching events, the audience could not always be certain that their prescience was totally accurate. This is the case in *Contra valor no hay desdicha,* when the ghost of the protagonist's foster father materializes in order to warn his son not to engage in combat with the King:

La voz:	*Ciro, no esperes al Rey.*
	Huye, que es mejor que huyas
	que no que la vida pierdas.
Ciro:	*Mucho mi valor injurias.*
	¿Quién eres?
La voz:	*Tu padre soy.* (*Acad.* VI, 313b)

Voice:	Cyrus, don't wait for the King.
	Flee, for it is better to flee
	than to lose your life.
Cyrus:	You mock my courage.
	Who are you?
Voice:	I am your father.

But Cyrus refuses to flee from the King's attacking army:

Ciro:	*Vete, sombra, á tu descanso,*
	vive la fúnebre tumba

de hombre vil, pues no mereces
como rey doradas urnas.
La voz: *Grandes desdichas te aguardan.*
Ciro: *Mientras que la vida dura,*
contra valor no hay desdicha.

(*Acad.* VI, 313b)

Cyrus: Away with you, ghost, go to your rest,
[You belong] in the funereal tomb
of a disgraced man, for you do not deserve
a king's golden urn.
Voice: Great misfortune awaits you.
Cyrus: As long as life goes on,
courage will never bring misfortune.

Although one would assume that members of the world beyond should have special knowledge of the world below, it turns out that the *sombra's* prediction was untrue even so. An *hombre vil* on earth, then, does not necessarily undergo a personality change once he has passed away, so we see that the ghost's prediction was not based on special knowledge but on the dictates of his own pusillanimous heart. The spectators, however, were still kept in suspense since they did not know whether the ghost's prediction would come true or not. Certainly the majority of Lope's ghosts demonstrate accurate foreknowledge, but this play is a curious example of the exception to that rule. In the more extensive analysis below, I shall try to show that the devices of foreshadowing were sometimes used by Lope not for the purpose of helping the spectators foresee the ending, but rather for the ironic goal of throwing them completely off the track.

In conclusion, then, it appears that Lope's use of the vocal *sombras* varied from mere entertainment to purposeful dramatic strategy. When *sombras* were sent on special missions to apprise the living of the needs of the dead, the results were necessarily undramatic. But when Lope had the *sombras* confront the characters with portents and warnings of doom, then the audience began to watch in fascination as the protagonist faced death with a heroic courage based on his sense of honor and on his moral convictions. Caupolicán fought for the freedom of his country and died with the knowledge of his own spiritual victory; the Duke of Viseo died in order not to betray his king. In both cases the hero had foreknowledge of what awaited him, but each was able to accept death as the only means of defending his honor, which was more important to him than life itself. In each play the audience was able to share the protagonist's fore-knowledge, but instead of witnessing a tragic inner struggle that eventually led the victim to his doom (as in the case of passionate love), the spectators felt the sort of awe that was often inspired by the lives of epic heroes who fought and died for a noble ideal.

OMENS

It goes without saying that literature provides us with many examples of prophecies or predictions of future occurrences voiced by spirits of the dead. One has only to remember the ghosts of the *Odyssey* and the *Aeneid* who foretell the future, or the souls who apprise Dante of things yet to come, or the predictions of the archangel Michael in *Paradise Lost.* The ancients, of course, were the first to acquaint us with the many devices of foreshadowing that appeared with such fre-quency in Lope's theatre, for omens, prophetic dreams, visions, and portents of every kind were common in their literature. It was Prometheus who first disclosed to mankind the art of divination, a gift which infuriated the gods, for they always hated to see mortals striving to transcend their neces-sary limitations. A passage from Aeschylus's play describes the kind of knowledge that Prometheus bestowed on man:

Prometheus:
*It was I who arranged all the ways of seercraft, and
I first adjudged what things come verily true from
dreams; and to men I gave meaning to the ominous
cries, hard to interpret. It was I who set in order the
omens of the highway and the flight of the crooked-
taloned birds, which of them were propitious or
lucky by nature...*[33]

But the chorus is quick to remind him that "the plans of
men shall never/ pass the ordered law of Zeus" (p. 223), for
Prometheus can do no more than teach man to *interpret* signs
and portents, whereas it remains the unique domain of the
gods themselves to have certain knowledge of the future.
One is led to conclude, then, that the gift of Prometheus in-
cites man to struggle against the will of the gods and to
challenge his fate in spite of his incomplete knowledge, and
this defiance makes him a potentially heroic figure as well as
a tragic one.[34]

An abiding interest in divination has filtered down
through the ages and has manifested itself particularly in the
popular literature of both Western and Eastern civilizations.
The general public in all countries is naturally infected by
both oral and written tradition, and the people living during
the Spanish Golden Age were certainly no exception. Lope's
audience was usually quite superstitious about the meaning
of various natural phenomena which were often interpreted

---

[33] *Prometheus Bound,* from *The Complete Greek Tragedies,* vol. I, ed.
David Grene and Richmond Lattimore, New York (Random House),
1942, p. 220.

[34] For a complete and well-documented list of many instances in which
supernatural phenomena occur in both ancient and modern literature, see
The Great Ideas: A Syntopicon of Great Books of the Western World (54
vols.), Robert Maynard Hutchins, editor in chief, Encyclopedia Britannica Inc., 1952, vol. II, chap. 72 ("Prophecy"), pp. 454-471.

as being indicative of good or bad fortune. The popularity of such conjectures was naturally reflected in the Golden Age theatre, where talk of omens, dreams, and portents abound.

El mejor mozo de España
("The Best Lad in Spain")

Lope, always interested in keeping his spectators entertained by treating them to liberal doses of marvels and magic,[35] was especially witty in the way he handled a cryptic note given to the young Ferdinand by a witch in *El mejor mozo de España.* The note, which was meant to predict the future of Ferdinand and Isabel, showed the letters *F* and *I* both covered with crowns. The audience knew immediately the significance of both the letters and the crowns,[36] but Ferdinand's friend Fadrique, having established that the *F* stood for *Fernando,* assigned erroneous meanings to the *I,* such as *iniquidad, infelicidad, infame, injuria, ira,* and the like ("iniquity, unhappiness, infamy, invective, ire").[37]

The spectators undoubtedly enjoyed these verbal ironies which suggested disasters that would never come about, for they knew by heart the history of Ferdinand and Isabel and the victorious future that awaited them. Isabel's vision in the first scene of the play was probably also designed to win

---

[35] For an extensive catalog of such phenomena, see Miguel Herrero and Manuel Cardenal, "Sobre los agüeros en la literatura española del siglo de oro," *RFE,* XXVI (1942), pp. 15-41.

[36] A play on words which Lapesa helps to clarify in the following observation: "En cuanto al aragonés, eran patentes al principio de esta época sus diferencias con el habla de Castilla: la hierba *hinojo* sirvió de símbolo a la unión de los dos reinos, porque, al decir de un poeta, "llámala Castilla *inojo,*/que es su letra I̲sabel; /llámala Aragón *finojo,*/ que es su letra de F̲ernando." *Historia de la lengua española,* Madrid, 1955, p.188. Lope was perhaps elaborating on this popular verbal symbolism.

[37] Ed. Aguilar, vol. III, p. 1043a.

cheers from the audience, for it showed her expelling the Jews and the Moors and achieving unity for her country. Even though Lope foreshadowed the ending by his use of these and other devices, the audience was able to contain its potential *cólera* because of its enthusiasm for the Catholic monarchs.

Belief in omens, however, was sternly censured by the authorities of the Church,[38] and Lope hardly ever missed an opportunity to add strong words of disapproval to the various speeches of the *graciosos,* confidants, and sundry friends of the character to whom these portents of doom were revealed. Even though the agonist himself is usually torn between his superstitious fear of the omen and his conscious desire not to believe in it, the audience is forewarned of impending doom by its appearance in the play, for in the majority of cases that have been studied in this thesis, the evil predicted by the omen turned out to be true[39] in spite of the skepticism of those who voiced the orthodox position.

El marqués de Mantua
("The Marquis of Mantua")

There is a good example of this ironic interplay of superstitious fear and orthodox skepticism in *El marqués de Mantua.* During the first act we learn that Prince Carloto, aided

---

[38] Otis Green (*Spain and the Western Tradition,* II, 233-234) uses illustrations from Hernando de Talavera, *Breve forma de confesar;* Juan del Encina, *Cancionero* (1496); Cristóbal de Villalón, *Diálogo de las transformaciones,* and several other sources to support this statement.

[39] I know of only two exceptions to this general rule: in *Contra valor no hay desdicha* Cyrus ignores a comet and kills his fallen horse in order to prove that he can conquer omens with strength and courage; and in *El conde Fernán González* the hero ignores the fact that one of his soldiers was swallowed up by the earth, thus proving the same point. Both these plays will be discussed more fully later on.

and abetted by the treacherous Galalón, is plotting to kill the noble Valdovinos so he can rape his fiancée, Sevilla. The Prince invites Valdovinos to go hunting with him, but Sevilla is troubled by mysterious forebodings, so she begs her lover not to go. Valdovinos pays no attention to what he considers to be her womanly fears and fancies, so the audience must watch with apprehension as he unknowingly takes the first steps toward a danger of which only they are aware.

It is not until the second act, however, that the audience realizes that the dangerous hunting expedition will almost certainly bring about the death of Valdovinos, for as he leaves his house he trips on the threshold and soon afterward he drops his sword. His servant is frightened by these bad omens and he goes on to describe a whole series of ominous events that have recently taken place, but Valdovinos refuses to pay any attention to his forebodings:

> *No tengo por buen Cristiano*
> *hombre que mira en agüeros.*
> *Saca el bayo, porque suba*
> *donde Sevilla me vea;*
> *que no habrá mal que lo sea,*
> *con reliquias desta aljuba.*
>
> (*Aguilar*, II, 1477b)

("A good Christian should never pay any attention to omens. Bring me the bay horse so I can go up there where Sevilla can see me; for the relics of this jubbah [Arabic garment] are not going to cause any evil.")

Soon afterward Valdovinos dies by the Prince's sword, so the portents of doom turn out to be true after all. The irony of the situation is quite clear to the audience, which is left with the feeling that if Valdovinos had been less of a *buen cristiano* and had been a little more leery of the relics, he would not have met with such an unhappy end.[40]

El bastardo Mudarra
("Mudarra the Illegitimate")

This play offers yet another example of the ironic interplay of superstitious fear and orthodox skepticism, when old Nuño Salido sees what he interprets to be bad omens. He tells the seven brothers to turn back from their foray against the enemy, but they are annoyed by his unchivalrous and unchristian attitude, and they refuse to listen to him.

Catholic orthodoxy, however, was not the only factor involved in the leading brother's decision to disregard the warnings of doom; of equal importance to him was his concern for his *honra*. The word *vergüenza* ("shame") is a term that associates itself with the idea of dishonor, and Nuño is quick to deny that he would compromise their honor in any way.[41] Belief in omens, then, is not only a sin in the eyes of the Church, but it is also a shameful weakness which

---

[40] Otis Green cites an interesting example of this subtle irony: "Céspedes y Meneses, in *El español Gerardo,* causes a character to give a plus-minus, or rather a minus-plus importance to omens: '*I omit telling of certain omens which I had on that day, because I have never been fearful of such things; but I assure you that if I had heeded them, and that if, when my horse stumbled in the center of a flowery meadow as I left town, dumping himself and his rider on the ground, I had really turned back as I was tempted to do, I should never have fallen into the cruel hands of my enemies.'" Spain and the Western Tradition,* vol. II, p. 237.

[41] He also means, at the same time, that to draw back from battle is shameful in itself, so that to allow oneself to be dissuaded from fighting because of bad omens is an act of cowardice. This attitude, of course, is shared by heroes throughout literature. See, for example, Diomede's fear of being thought a coward for fleeing Hector's troops after Jove sent him a bad omen. *Iliad,* Book VIII, p. 52b in the Great Books edition.

threatens to strip an individual of his honor in the eyes of society.

Reichenberger has pointed out the inseparable relationship between honor and faith: "The two rocks on which the whole idealogical system of the *Comedia* is built are *la honra* and *la fe*. *La honra* upholds the individual as a social being, *la fe* sustains him when he faces the enigma of man's position on earth. *La honra* and *la fe* are indissolubly bound together for the Spaniard of the Golden Age. Upholding the faith was an intimate part of national and personal honor."[42]

The conscious decision on the part of the protagonists to go forward into battle despite the warnings of the omens serves to heighten the dramatic tension and to underscore the courage and the rectitude of the characters. But this play is clearly not tragic; the brothers are innocent victims of Ruy Velázquez and Doña Lambra, who are in turn slain for their crime by Mudarra. It is a melodrama of villains and victims, revenge and satisfaction, in which the central characters do not struggle with inner dilemmas or with an inexorable fate.

Although the spectators were well acquainted with the popular legend and were aware of the fate that awaited the brothers, the discussion of omens nevertheless drove home the irony of the situation as they watched the unknowing victims on their way to the slaughter. Lope's rational, well-meaning advice against giving credence to the omens was dutifully taken by Nuño, whose faith and honor caused him to renounce immediately any fears that might have been based on "shameful" beliefs.

The audience finds itself in the awkward position of wishing that Nuño would be a little more "shameful" and heed the warning of the omens, but at the same time we know the characters are destined to be forever ignorant of

---

[42] Arnold Reichenberger, "The Uniqueness of the *Comedia*," *HR*, XXVII (1959), p. 308.

what lies ahead. This time Sedgewick's definition of dramatic irony applies perfectly to the situation: "The spectator in the theatre always sees and knows both the appearance and the reality; and he senses the contradiction between what the ignorant character *does* and what he *would* do."[43]

El amigo por fuerza
("The Friend by Obligation")

Lope's advice to the spectators may have been well-meaning in *El bastardo Mudarra,* but an extraordinary example of a case in which the skeptical character shows real hypocrisy occurs in *El amigo por fuerza,* when the *alcalde* (the mayor) tells Lisaura that he had been frightened by a nightmare. She responds with contempt:

> *Es loco el que agüeros toma;*
> *que todos suelen salir*
> *mil veces por lo contrario.* (*Acad N* III, 275b)

("One has to be crazy to believe in omens; they tend to come out exactly the opposite way a thousand times over.")

Having stated her position in no uncertain terms, one minute later she and another lady stab him to death while making a jail-break. The irony here is twofold: Lisaura knows quite well that she is the reason for his fear, even though she pretends not to know what is in store for him... yet although she accuses him of being crazy to believe that he is in danger, she herself proves that he is right by killing him.

The *alcalde* is in the same peculiar double bind as all the other agonists who are confronted with omens, for if he believes in the omen he will be considered superstitious and

---

[43] G. G. Sedgewick, *Of Irony...* p.49. See also p.22 of the intro above.

"shameful," but if he pays no attention to it he will be proven wrong. It is important to note, however, that in this play the *alcalde* is a villainous figure (among his many transgressions he stands accused of having wanted to seduce the ladies who were disguised as slaves), so his death comes by way of punishment and is no doubt greeted with enthusiastic applause. His ironic double bind, then, offers the spectators one more reason to boo him, for they were only too ready to believe he was superstitious, shameful, and misguided. He is not a hero caught in a tragic dilemma—he is a scoundrel mocked.

El príncipe despeñado
("The Prince Who Was Hurled From a Cliff")

We find a similar irony in *El príncipe despeñado* when King[44] Sancho's majordomo Martín advises him not to pay attention to omens. The passage is imbued with irony, for the audience knows that Martín is about to kill King Sancho for violating his wife. But the King, although he expresses forebodings about what the future might hold, is nevertheless totally ignorant of the fact that his own majordomo will be the instrument of his doom, so almost everything he says in this passage becomes ironic, starting with the affectionate "*Martín/ de mis ojos y de mi alma.*" Martín's speech is no less ironic as he reassures the King that he has nothing to fear, then both the audience and the majordomo ironically watch him as he confidently approaches the cliff from which he is about to be hurled. But despite his partial awareness he is too much of a villain (at least according to the prrevailing honor code) to be considered a tragic figure.[45]

---

[44] Sancho was acclaimed King when he was still only fifteen years old.

[45] The case of a character killing a man of higher rank than himself in order to avenge his honor occurs with some frequency in Lope's plays, the most obvious example being found in *Peribáñez.* Many critics have

El último godo
("The Last Goth")

This is also the case in *El último godo,* as the main characters are traitors to their country and therefore cannot be expected to elicit the sympathy of the audience. The play is nevertheless brimming with devices that foreshadow the ending, even though the legend is so popular that the spectators do not need to be reminded of the fate that awaits the villains. One must assume that the audience is greatly entertained by the irony of Rodrigo's gross misinterpretations of the bad omens that befall him. When his crown spontaneously falls off his head, the King decides to interpret the meaning of this event to suit himself.[46]

In the second act Rodrigo dreams that a hound barked at him and grabbed him by the coat, but this time the verbal irony is provided by his wife, who assures him that he has no reason to be melancholy. She gives rational explanations for his dream, and reminds him that it is sacrilegious to believe in omens. He dies soon afterward, however, so the omens concerning him are fulfilled

---

discussed the two aspects of honor that can be distinguished in the *Comedia:* exterior honor which is based on reputation and heredity, and interior honor, based on personal virtue. In this play Lope makes it clear that although the King has exterior honor due to his noble rank, he is still devoid of interior honor because he cannot respect the rights of others. Hence his punishment is justified, and Don Martín is exonerated. For studies on the honor theme, see Américo Castro, "Algunas observaciones acerca del honor en los siglos XVI y XVII," *RFE,* III (1916), pp.1-50, *idem, De la edad conflictiva,* Chapter I: "El drama de la honra en España y en su literatura," Madrid, 1961; Ramón Menéndez Pidal, *De Cervantes y Lope de Vega,* "Del honor en el teatro español," Madrid (Austral), 1940; García Valdecasas, *El hidalgo y el honor,* Madrid, 1948; Valbuena Prat, *Historia del teatro español,* Chapter XV, Barcelona, 1956.

[46] This is an old theme. Alexander and Caesar, two examples among many, both misinterpreted bad omens. See The Great Books edition of *Plutarch's Lives,* p. 568a,b and 575a (Alexander); 601d-604d (Caesar).

Julián's fate is even more terrifying: at the beginning of the second act he tells the Moors that his daughter's first words were *nací para mal de España* ("I was born to the great detriment of Spain," p. 641b). He also mentions that when she was just a small child she had many dreams about death and ghosts, and that an astrologer had told him that she would commit suicide by throwing herself off a tower. This time Lope is using omens, nightmares, and dreadful predictions to torture the villainous agonist, much to the delight of the spectators, who must have taken great satisfaction in seeing the wicked get their just deserts, a response appropriate to the essentially melodramatic nature of the play. The prediction about Florinda soon comes true, and in the third act Julián's wife dies of cancer. After facing the grief of losing his whole family, Julián himself is killed as a traitor by the very Moors he had sought to benefit—the final irony.

El conde Fernán González
("Count Ferdinand Gonzalez")

Although we may smile, perhaps, at the irony involved in Rodrigo's blind and foolish misinterpretations of what it meant to have dropped his crown and scepter, not all omens are necessarily as bad as they seem at first sight. In *El conde Fernán González* there is a good example of just how deceptive so-called omens can be: as the Count is rallying his men to make an attack on Almanzor's army, one of them is suddenly and mysteriously swallowed up by the earth. The remaining soldiers are terrified by what they take to be a bad omen, interpreting it to mean that they will surely die. This time Fernán González does not attempt to suggest that it was somehow a natural phenomenon, since it would obviously be impossible to do so, but instead he interprets the omen as he sees fit, saying that his soldiers are so strong that they cause the very earth to cave in under them (*Acad.* VII, 422a). He somehow manages to make his soldiers believe this interpretation, and shortly thereafter it is corroborated by the famous victory. A virtuous, God-fearing hero, then, can overcome by his own faith and bravery whatever evil may be indicated by bad omens. A wicked character, however, is bound to be the victim of his own self-deception if he decides to disregard or misinterpret the omens according to his personal desires.

We have seen that Lope took pains to foreshadow the death of innocent victims (*El bastardo Mudarra, El marqués de Mantua*), foolish scoundrels (*El amigo por fuerza*), lecherous kings (*El príncipe despeñado*), and villainous traitors (*El último godo*). But these plays did not produce tragic figures, for the characters were either too virtuous or else too sinful. The foreshadowing, however, was used to very good advantage in that it allowed the audience to enjoy the various forms of dramatic irony that developed as a result of the discrepancies existing between the different interpretations suggested by the omens to the audience and to the characters, as well as discrepancies resulting from the events themselves as they appeared to the characters and as they were known to the spectators, and from the foreknowledge of the audience as compared to the ignorance of the characters.

The most curious irony of all lies in the fact that the characters, because of their religious convictions, did not permit themselves to heed the omens which were warning them of an impending misfortune. If they had paid attention to the omens they might have avoided the misfortune, but it appears that God wishes them to continue on the pathway to doom by forbidding them to believe the handwriting on the wall. This might be a good argument for the intricate workings of divine justice were it not for the fact that God allows both the guilty and the innocent to fall into the very traps that the omens are warning them to avoid. While it is true that God's will is inscrutable, it is probably more to the point for us to keep in mind what has already been said about Lope's dramatic purpose in using his arsenal of omens, for his plays would have been less effective if the audience had not had foreknowledge of the fate of the characters. The spectators are thus able to survey the action on the stage from an ironic, "Godlike" distance, aware that the characters are doomed for good or for evil to fulfill their individual destinies, and aware too, perhaps, that we are all rather vulnerable creatures in an existence whose paradoxes and contradictions we can sometimes sense but never fully comprehend.

DREAMS

When nightmares are interpreted by the dreamer as a portent of doom, they are treated with the same mistrust as the bad omens based on natural phenomena. Typical of the reactions they elicit from other characters in the play is the Queen's speech in *El último godo:*

> *Señor mío, no habéis*
> *de hacer los sueños verdad*
> *contra la fidelidad*
> *que a vuestra fe le debéis...*
>
> *(Acad.* VII, 94a)

("My Lord, you should not believe in dreams that are contrary to your faith...")

Yet despite the skepticism voiced by the other characters, the evil predicted by the dream invariably comes true.[47] Thus Ruy Velázquez is tormented by nightmares of the seven murdered brothers just before Mudarra slays him *(El bastardo Mudarra)*, the a*lc*alde (mayor) dreams he is turned into a

---

[47] I am still excluding the exceptional *Contra valor no hay desdicha,* and the other two plays of the same theme: *Lo que ha de ser* and *Lo que está determinado.*

serpent just minutes before Lisaura stabs him *(El amigo por fuerza)*, Don Juan dreams he is being chased by a bull, and Don Pedro dreams he was thrown off a high tower shortly before they are both *despeñados (La inocente sangre)*. *Corta vida y triste muerte,/soñaba yo que tenía* ("I dreamed I would have a short life and a sad death"), says Adonis just before he dies[48], and Bamba foresees his own death in a dream which shortly afterward turns out to be true *(La comedia de Bamba)*. It is noteworthy that these nightmares about death all occur immediately before the dreamer is actually killed, so in these cases Lope is using the devices of foreshadowing merely to heighten the dramatic intensity of the moment, rather than using them as a way to prepare the audience, right from the beginning, for a tragic *dénouement* in which the protagonist is perceived to be a hero caught inevitably in the web of his own destiny.

El ganso de oro
("The Golden Goose")

Occasionally a dream is used not only to forewarn the protagonist of coming danger, but also to help him to avoid the traps that are being set for him. In *El ganso de oro* Belardo has a dream in which the "gran Sirena" warns him that Silvero will try to kill him:

> *Despierta, que te quieren dar la muerte,*
> *sin que la veas, a traición un hombre*
> *que es de tu misma tierra y de tu sangre.*
> *Pero toma este anillo, que sin duda*
> *verás con él la daga, ya que sea*
> *ver al traidor tan imposible caso.*
> (*Acad. N.*, I, 181a)

---

[48] *Adonis y Venus*, Aguilar 563a

("Wake up, for a treacherous man from your own land and of
your own blood wants to kill you without your seeing it
coming. Take this ring, for with it you will certainly see the
dagger, even though it will be impossible for you to see the
traitor himself.")

Although the warning comes too close to the end of the
play to count as "authentic" foreshadowing (i.e. of the kind
that would affect its entire dramatic structure), the audience
is curious to find out what it will be like for Belardo to deal
with a man who is invisible to him, thanks to the wiles of a
scheming magician.

What follows is an absolutely graphic example of irony,
for the spectators can actually *see* Silvero as he moves about
the stage, while at the same time he is invisible to Belardo
and to the other characters. The stage business performed by
Silvero before he draws his dagger (which was visible to
Belardo because of the magic ring) must have been both
entertaining and effective: one can imagine how he might
have attempted to choke or hit his victim instead of stabbing
him while the audience looked on in suspense, fearing that if
he fails to draw his dagger his presence will not be known to
Belardo in time. Here the ironic conflict between appearance
and reality is literally being acted out right before the very
eyes of the audience.

In the hagiographic plays the dreams can usually be
interpreted as messages sent to the dreamer by God.[49] The
Old Testament is full of prophecies of this kind, for "Where
pagan prognosticators may claim to be divinely inspired in
the sense of having special powers of interpretation, the
Hebrew prophets speak from a different kind of supernatural

---

[49] See C.E. Aníbal, "Voces del Cielo: A Note on Mira de Amescua," *RR,*
XVI (1925), and *idem,* "Another Note on the *Voces del Cielo, RR,* XVIII
(1927).

inspiration. They are the vessels through which the Lord Himself speaks. They are interpreters only in that they make known to others what God has made known to them."[50]

La hermosa Ester
("The Beautiful Esther")

Sometimes the prophecies predicted doom and destruction, accompanied by moral instruction and warnings to remember God's laws. But usually the tidings were favorable to the virtuous and to the persecuted, showing that the good shall be rewarded for their kindness and humility. Thus, in *La hermosa Ester,* Mardoqueo tells Isaac about a dream he has had concerning his people: Against a confusing background of thunder, lightning, and ferocious dragons, he sees a vision of two armies mercilessly attacking a defenseless multitude. But then a small fountain turns into a raging river, the storm abates, and finally the innocents triumph. The good Mardoqueo correctly interprets the meaning of the dream:

> *Yo pienso que ha de ser para bien nuestro,*
> *aunque ha de ser por medio de mil penas;*
> *mas como al sol precede oscura noche,*
> *así la gloria de las penas sale.*

(*Aguilar*, 112b)

("I think it must be for our own good, though it come by means of a thousand troubles; but just as dark night precedes the sun, in the same way glory bursts forth from pain.")

The meaning of the dream (which does not appear in the Book of Esther) is even clearer to the spectator familiar with the story as it is told in the Bible, for it is well known that the

---

[50] *The Great Ideas...(op.cit.)* p. 458a. For a list of all the dreams, visions, and visitations in the Old Testament, the Apocrypha, and the New Testament, see p. 466.

Jews were delivered from their would-be assailants through the intervention of Esther. In introducing this dream, then, Lope strengthens the audience's foreknowledge and heightens the irony of the drama. The biblical tale itself describes several ironical situations which Lope uses to full advantage in his theatrical presentation. Since the righteous protagonists need an evil force to provide dramatic tension, the King's adviser Amán soon emerges as the antagonist, and the main irony of the play begins to center itself around his unhappy fate. As in the other villain/victim plays mentioned above, the audience enjoys watching the wicked adviser suffering punishments for his arrogance and cold egotism. When the King asks him to name a suitable reward for one who has served him well, Amán assumes he is referring to him, so he suggests that the man in question be dressed in the King's clothes and paraded around the city on the King's horse.

But the spectators know that the King has Mardoqueo in mind for this reward, so they are highly entertained by the irony inherent in Amán's ignorance of the King's intentions, and in the fact that Mardoqueo, who would not deign to kneel at Amán's feet, is the last person in the world that the recalcitrant adviser would like to see in a position of honor. Equally ironic is the fact that Amán is finally condemned to death on the very gallows that he had constructed for the execution of Mardoqueo, whom he had unjustly accused of treachery.

These ironic situations, as well as the many innuendoes, understatements, hidden meanings, and other examples of verbal irony which may be found in almost every scene of the play, all serve to illustrate the underlying quotation from the Bible twice repeated by the chorus-like musicians:

> *Dios ensalza los humildes*
> *y derribe los soberbios.*
>
> (*Aguilar,* 127b, 128a)

("God raises up the humble and throws down the proud.")

This pronouncement is, of course, essentially the same as the conclusions already drawn about the meaning of Mardoqueo's dream. Thus the events fulfill the predictions of the prophetic dream, and Mardoqueo's interpretation, inspired by God's grace, is proven correct.

Los trabajos de Jacob
("The Travails of Jacob")

Another example of dreams being interpreted correctly is to be found in *Los trabajos de Jacob,* significantly subtitled *Sueños hay que verdad son* ("Some Dreams are True"). In this play, however, Lope is scrupulously faithful to the biblical text (as he is in most of his hagiographic plays), using the dreams and their interpretations as they appear in Genesis: Jacob's youngest son Joseph is sold to some Ishmaelite traders by his jealous brothers. Pharaoh buys him from the traders and takes him to his palace, where Pharaoh's wife Potifar tries to seduce him. When Joseph turns her down she complains to Pharaoh that he made unseemly advances, so Pharaoh puts him in prison. Joseph has a dream about some sheaves of wheat that stand upright and are surrounded by the sheaves of his brothers lying on the ground; this he interprets as meaning that he will some day rule over his brothers (Gen: 37:5-7). Later Joseph correctly interprets the dreams of some of his fellow prisoners, one of whom will be honored by Pharaoh, while the other will be decapitated (Gen: 40:8-22).

Finally God blesses Pharaoh's house for Joseph's sake, allowing him to interpret some puzzling dreams of Pharaoh's whose meaning had persistently eluded all the magicians and even the wisest men of Egypt: in one dream seven fat cows are devoured by seven lean cows, and in the other dream seven good ears of corn are eaten by seven bad ears. Joseph warns Pharaoh that after seven plentiful years there will be a seven-year famine, and he advises him to make provisions for this disaster (Gen 41:1-40). When his interpretation comes true, Pharaoh honors him by placing him in charge of his entire household.

This Old Testament story offers Lope a ready-made plot for his theatrical presentation, complete with dramatic irony and devices of foreshadowing. The audience or reader is made aware of the impending action through Joseph's predictions which they know will come true not only because they know the Bible, but also because it is made thoroughly clear that the protagonist is inspired by God (*Acad.* III, 245a). But this time the dramatic irony does not function in quite the same way as it did in most of the other plays that we have studied so far, because there exists here a small but important difference: the protagonist has certain knowledge of the outcome of the events, and hence shares with the audience their ironic, "God-like" distance. Joseph is aware of his divine inspiration, and he knows that what he foresees will certainly come true for this reason. His foreknowlege, then, prevents him from being an ironic figure himself, for there is within him no conflict between appearance and reality. He sees reality as we see it, he knows the outcome as we know it, he is not unwittingly fooled by circumstances he only half understands; instead, he controls his fate because he knows he is the instrument of God's will.

The real irony, however, lies in the behavior of the ten brothers who are all unaware (although forewarned) of how the action will eventually lead to the fulfillment of Joseph's predictions. They believed that they could rid themselves of him forever by selling him as a slave to the Ishmaelites, but both Joseph and the audience know that he is destined to be anything but a slave. Their belief that they can thus mold their own lives according to their personal wishes is made to look pathetic and foolish in the light of what we know about

God's plan for Joseph's people. The rest of the main plot bears this out as we ironically watch the brothers do as they are told by Pharaoh's chief adviser, for they are entirely ignorant of the identity of the adviser until the final scene of Recognition, when they understand at last that Joseph's prophecies have come true.

The futility of man's egotistic efforts to force his circumstances to fit his own personal desire is echoed in the subplot,[51] when the rustic Bato tries to compel the disdainful Lida to love him by threatening to make known her love for Benjamin, the youngest son of Jacob.[52] Lida is so worried that Bato might reveal her intimate secret that she pretends to "love" him against her will, but he finds her false love dissatisfying even so.[53] A similar situation occurs in the main plot when Nicela insists on loving Joseph even though he cannot return her feelings. Her guilty and one-sided love is alse recounted in the Bible version, but Lope adds a touch of his own in the last scene when he has Joseph forgive Nicela. All those characters, then, who have tried in vain to alter God's plan are finally brought to understand their foolishness; their new understanding causes them to feel contrition, and through contrition comes forgiveness.

---

[51] See Diego Marín, *La intriga secundaria en el teatro de Lope de Vega*, Toronto (Univ. of Toronto Press), 1958. Although Marín points out that the subplots of Lope's hagiographic, legendary, and historical plays are generally independent of the main action, we find here a thematic unity between plot and subplot which serves to highlight the central meaning of the play.

[52] There is an amusing irony in Lida's angry words to Bato: *¿Pues qué necedad más fría/ que amar a quien te aborrece?* Acad. III, 246b ("What is more idiotic than to love someone who despises you?"). She seems to be unaware that she is committing the same *necedad* ("idiocy") in loving Benjamin, who "knows nothing of love" according to the frustrated Lida (246a).

[53] The influence of astrology and the stars on the fate of passionate lovers will be examined at greater length in Part Three.

The two hagiographic plays we have just studied both serve to illustrate a special use of dramatic irony, but despite the many cases of foreshadowing that occur in the religious plays, they are nevertheless generally devoid of irony since the God-given knowledge of the protagonists is accepted by them without question or doubt. Like Joseph, they are neither ignorant, nor half-aware, nor self-deceptive but fully conscious of God's will, announced to them by His messengers. There is no discrepancy, then, between their knowledge and that of the audience, so there is no dramatic irony except in the case of the ignorant characters who do not share the foreknowledge of the protagonists and of the spectators.

KLEDONOMANCY

We have seen that dramatic irony is present when reality as it appears to the characters in the play is radically different from the audience's interpretation of that same reality, and Lope employs a great variety of devices to communicate foreknowledge to the spectators as well as forebodings to the ignorant or semi-ignorant characters.

One of the strangest of these is a phenomenon know as kledonomancy,[54] a term used by the ancient Greeks to describe the misinterpretation of stray words (overheard by chance) as having great bearing on a critical situation, when in reality the words have no connection at all to the particular situation. This phenomenon is well known to psychiatrists today as a symptom of paranoia or schizophrenia. According to Alan A. Stone and Sue Smart Stone, "schizophrenic patients often misinterpret the events in the world around

---

[54] This word derives from the Greek *klēdōn*, meaning "a chance or casual utterance that contains an omen, or is assumed to."

them. One method of misinterpretation is so common that it has been given a special designation: ideas of reference. A patient suffering with ideas of reference believes that every irrelevant or coincidental action or happening in the world around him is related to him, caused by him, or arranged for him. If strangers cross the street, it is to avoid him because they have been warned. If three men pass wearing hats, it was pre-arranged to show him that he is a fool for not wearing a hat. If all the traffic lights are red, it has been set up to test his restraint. If some passing stranger spits, it is meant to be a direct insult and challenge to his masculinity. Whispered conversation always refers to him, and laughter is inevitably directed at him."[55] A. H. Krappe summarizes the historical origins of the stage-technical device,[56] reminding us that kledonomancy occurred in Homer, Plutarch, Aristophanes, the Old Testament, *El poema del Cid, El cantar de los infantes de Lara,* and in the literatures of India and North Africa as well.

"To the Arabs of North Africa," he writes, "The same belief is familiar, ominous stray words of this character being called *fâl*" (p. 66). He later makes the interesting observation that the Arab domination in Spain might have contributed a good deal to the reenforcement of this superstitious belief in the minds of the Spanish people (p.67).

There can be little doubt that kledonomancy was well known in Spain during the Middle Ages and the Golden Age. C. E. Aníbal has this to say: "Alfonso X *el Sabio* had already condemned, among other evil practices of divination, the *agüero... de palabras a que llaman "proverbio"* ("the omen... fashioned by words which are called a "proverb"),

---

[55] *The Abnormal Personality Through Literature,* ed. Alan A. Stone and Sue Smart Stone, Prentice Hall, Inc., Englewood Cliffs, N. J., 1966.
[56] Alexander Haggerty Krappe, "Notes on the *Voces del Cielo," RR,* XVII (1926), 65-68.

declaring that those found guilty of this offense should be put to death... The explicitness of this *ley* and the severity of the penalty are evidence of an existing custom, the continued existence of which made it necessary for Juan II in 1410, and Felipe II in 1598, to penalize those officers of justice who failed to prosecute offenses or to exact the penalty already established by the *Partidas,* public readings of the law being now required on one market day of each month."[57]

Pedro Ciruelo, writing some seventy years prior to Lope's most productive period, describes the same phenomenon which he defines with the Latin word "omen".[58] One must bear in mind, however, that the messages given to the characters through the omens and dreams in Lope's theatre could almost always be interpreted as acts of God, for the characters were usually being warned of the dangers awaiting them if they did not take themselves in hand and face the truth of their situation.[59] Lope uses the omen to warn the misguided characters "as if it (the omen) were the word of God or of some good angel" (cf. footnote 57 below), which allows him to communicate directly with the spectators, the majority of whom must have believed in the current superstitions, and so the foreshadowing suggested by the omen often turned out to be exactly what the audience anticipated. The extraordinary irony here lies in the willingness of the charac-

---

[57] C.E. Aníbal, "Another Note on the *Voces del Cielo, RR,* XVIII (1927), p. 249. He mentions that both *proverbio* and *arfil* (or *alfil*) are defined by the *Diccionario de Autoridades* as referring to the phenomenon we are now calling kledonomancy, a term generally used by modern students of religion and folklore.

[58] Pedro Ciruelo, *Reprobación de las Supersticiones y Hechicerías* (1530), Madrid, 1952, p. 50.

[59] One can never safely generalize Lope's use of the devices of fore-shadowing into any set pattern or specific dramatic technique, for there do exist exceptions to his usual rules. In this section we shall study a case of kledonomancy which turns out *not* to indicate the character's true situation when we examine *El servir con mala estrella.*

ters themselves to interpret the omen as Ciruelo would have them do it, for as we have already seen, they constantly fear that such a belief is a mortal sin inspired by Satan. They refuse to listen to what turn out to be the *voces del cielo* (heavenly voices) and consequently they hurry all the faster down the road to their doom.[60]

Aníbal finds a good illustration of kledonomancy in *Don Quijote de la Mancha,*[61] where we find the same conflict between the desire to believe the omen and the fear that it is somehow foolish or sinful to do so. Green paraphrases the incident as follows:

"As Don Quijote approaches his village for the last time, unable now to accomplish the disenchantment of his lady Dulcinea, he overhears the voices of two quarrelling boys, one of whom shouts: *No te canses, Periquillo, que no la has de ver en todos los días de tu vida* (Part II, ch 73), ("Do not tire yourself, Periquillo, for you shall not see her again in all the days of your life.") The reference is to a cage *(una jaula)* of crickets, but the feminine pronoun *la* suggests to Don Quijote's depressed mind the enchanted lady of his thoughts and dreams. Sancho upbraids his master for coming up with such a superstitious interpretation, reminding him that the village condemns as silly all Christians who pay attention to such trifles… But this safeguard seems scarcely necessary, for the reader sees more clearly than Sancho and realizes that Don Quijote is being led and admonished by a genuine voice from heaven." (*Spain,* II, p. 238)

Whether or not the boy's words are really a message from heaven does not concern us here; but Sancho's attitude

---

[60] Green mentions several other Golden Age dramatists who use the device of kledonomancy as an example of God's will (*Spain* II, pp. 237-239). But since there seems to be no evidence that Lope is interested in making this a theological problem, I shall discuss only the dramatic aspects of this technique.

[61] "Another Note on the *Voces del Cielo,*" pp. 247-248.

is typical of the many skeptical characters that we have encountered in Lope's theatre, who warn the protagonists *not*
to listen to the omens. If the protagonists *had* listened to
them, there would have been no conflict and no dramatic
irony. The reader and the audience must see more clearly
than the characters, but the drama is heightened when the
characters are only semi-aware themselves.

La inocente sangre
("Innocent Blood")

An excellent example of kledonomancy in Lope's theatre
occurs in *La inocente sangre,* when Don Juan is in the act of
declaring his love to Doña Ana. Suddenly he hears the voice
of a gardener who interrupts his declaration by saying, "¿Tan
temprano lleváis flor? Tarde gozaréis del fruto" (*Acad.* IX,
182b), ("Are you blossoming so early? Then it will be late
when you enjoy the fruit.") Don Juan is upset by what seems
to be the gardener's cruel prediction concerning his love, but
Ana insists on the rational explanation: the gardener is only
talking to a tree, and there is no connection at all between his
prediction and Don Juan's future. Then, just as he asks Ana
to give him her word that she will marry him, the voice of
the gardener is heard again saying that he swears he will not
see her again for the rest of his life: "Yo os juro que no os
veáis/ en vuestra vida con ella..." The words have now
become intolerable to Don Juan, and he asks the gardener for
an explanation. It turns out the gardener was indeed talking
to a tree that had bloomed too early in the season and was
therefore in danger of losing its first fruit to the frost. He
then repeats the whole soliloquy for Don Juan:

> *¿Tan temprano dais la flor?*
> *tarde gozaréis del fruto.*
> *aunque almendra dulce y bella*

prometéis, y en flores dais
tales esperanzas della,
yo os juro que no os veáis
en vuestra vida con ella.   (*Acad* IX, 182a)

("Are you blossoming so soon? It will be late when you bear fruit, then. Even though you promise to produce sweet and beautiful almonds, and although your flowers make this hope seem possible, I swear to you that never in all your life will you be with her [the feminine pronoun refers to the fruit].")

Don Juan has to admit that the gardener's explanation is perfectly reasonable, but he cannot entirely rid himself of the feeling that the words are somehow ominous.[62] Once again we are faced with a situation similar to those in which the characters react ambiguously to a dream or a natural phenomenon that appears to be a bad omen. On the one hand they fear the evil suggested by the omen, but at the same time they convince themselves (or they allow themselves to be convinced) that it is either unreasonable or even downright sacrilegious to pay credence to the warnings. Their inability to see their future clearly makes them, as we have often seen,

---

[62] C.E. Aníbal ("Another Note on the *Voces del Cielo*" p. 250) points out an example of kledonomancy in *La Celestina (Clásicos Castellanos,* vol. I, pp. 156-157). As Celestina left her house one morning she overheard a conversation in the street which happened to deal with *achaques de amores* ("love sickness"). This time the omen is used not to warn the lovers about the dangers of passion, but rather to inspire Celestina in her morally questionable enterprise, which provides a good illustration of Ciruelo's contention that whoever believes in such omens does so *por inspiración del diablo con quien tiene pacto secreto* ("through the inspiration of the Devil, with whom he has a secret pact."). There is humorous irony in her interpretation of the meaning of the omen which is good only from her own viewpoint, but not in terms of what we know of the destiny of the lovers.

ironic figures as we watch them heading for the disaster of which they themselves are only half aware.[63]

Don Juan's semi-awareness is evident to the audience throughout the play, but one of the most interesting pieces of verbal irony occurs at the end of the second act when the King, who had unjustly imprisoned Morata for the murder of a nobleman, suddenly frees the innocent suspect. Don Juan is delighted to see Morata again, saying that God smiles on the innocent (191a), but the audience knows, as the unfortunate Don Juan does not, that the King has seen fit to free Morata not because he is wise and just, but because he was foolish enough to be convinced (by some flimsy evidence given to him by envious counselors) that Don Juan and his brother were the guilty parties. So Don Juan's statement that God protects the innocent acquires an ironic significance in terms of our understanding of the King's character and our knowledge of the counselor's malicious plans. Another aspect of the irony inherent in his words is the fact that Don Juan cannot and will not see the evil which motivates the three antagonists, precisely because he himself is too virtuous to suspect them of treachery.

The ironic statement gathers further significance at the end of the play when the guilty King hears a voice that admonishes him for having killed the innocent brothers:[64]

---

[63] It is interesting to note that the gardener himself is ignorant of the double meaning of his own words, which adds to the irony of the situation a dimension not present in such plays as *El duque de Viseo*, where the "warning figure" is totally aware of the meaning of his *caveat*. This time the spectators are alone in their foreknowledge of the fate of the two young men—a foreknowledge not shared by any of the other characters in the play.

[64] Their premonitions concerning their own deaths which came to them through the various nightmares has already been discussed above.

Los que en la tierra juzgáis
mirad que los inocentes
están a cargo de Dios,
que siempre por ellos vuelve.
No os ciegue pasión ni amor:[65]
juzgad jurídicamente;
que quien castiga sin culpa,
a Dios la piedad ofende.

                                        (*Acad* IX, 205a)

("Be careful whom you judge on earth, for the innocent are in God's care. His face shines upon them, so do not let yourselves be blinded by passion or love. Judge fairly, for whoever punishes a blameless victim offends the piety of God.")

Later on the King and his counselors die a mysterious death, punished for their blind and sinful actions by God's justice. It is interesting that the foreshadowing of the play should have been centered around the doomed brothers rather than the King and his counselors. The latter were not unironic figures, however, for the audience was doubtless well acquainted with the legend of Fernando el Emplazado (Ferdinand the Summoned), so although the antagonists did not foresee their fate, the audience was fully expecting it.

El servir con mala estrella
("Serving Faithfully Despite Ill Fortune")

Kledonomancy does not always correctly foreshadow the ending of the play, however, as is evident in *El servir con mala estrella*. The noble Rugero serves King Alfonso to the best of his ability, showing at all times the greatest possible

---

[65] Here *pasión* is used in the sense of "prejudice," or "favoritism."

courage, loyalty, and courtesy, yet for some reason the King never rewards him for his exemplary service. But Rugero is not easily discouraged, even when the King confers lavish rewards on those knights who fought less bravely than he, for he feels certain that some sort of special recognition is being reserved for him.

His patience and humility finally diminish in the third act, however, especially when he overhears some musicians singing about the Cid, who also served his King faithfully but without reward—the singers compare him to a dog who meekly dies of starvation at his master's doorstep. Rugero immediately believes that the words of the song apply to him personally, so he contemplates leaving the King's service.

Later on he comes across King Alfonso playing chess with a Moorish potentate, and while he is hesitating nearby, he overhears the King say "checkmate" to the Moor. Once again Rugero believes that this somehow applies to him, and he takes it to be a bad omen. He tells Alfonso that he would like to leave his court, giving as his reason his conviction that he was born under an evil star and is therefore fated to go unrewarded no matter how hard he tries to merit fame and compensation for his virtue.

The King presents him with two coffers, stating that one is empty while the other is laden with jewels, and he asks the youth to choose one. Rugero selects the empty one, which further convinces him of his predestined ill-fortune. King Alfonso does not deny that some people have worse luck than others, but he opposes Rugero's belief in predestination. To prove that man is capable of overcoming what appears to be an evil fate, he kindly gives him not only the coffer of jewels but also the hand of the woman he loves.

The foreshadowing suggested by the musicians' song and the checkmating of the Moor spells doom for Rugero only when it is interpreted from his own self-interested point of view. But the spectators surely recall that the King finally rewards the Cid for his deeds, and they are also aware that the checkmating of the Moorish King means victory for the Christians. Once again we find that the irony of the play rests on the self-deception of a character who not only misinterprets the meaning of the devices of foreshadowing but also deceives himself into believing he is humble and virtuous, when in reality he is displaying these qualities to serve his own ambition and self-interest. The truly virtuous character is, of course, King Alfonso, who has absolutely nothing to gain by giving Rugero the coffer of jewels. Lope's purpose is to represent to the audience the belief that man can free himself from the so-called influence of the stars by serving God sincerely, with true humility and love.[66]

PROPHECIES

Just as God-given knowledge can occasionally be communicated to virtuous characters through dreams and omens in Lope's plays, the same holds true for divinely inspired prophecies that predict future events. Although such auguries occur mostly in the hagiographic plays, we shall see in the next section that they are not limited to that genre.[67]

---

[66] Part Two will be dedicated to a more complete study of the theme of free will and predestination in Lope's theatre. This particular play gives the theme a somewhat tricky and superficial treatment, however, so it is not one of the best examples.

[67] Once in a while an allegorical figure will appear in very early plays that still reflect the practices of the late sixteenth century. In *El nuevo mundo descubierto por Cristóbal Colón* (1598? - 1603), *Imaginación* appears before Colón and tells him that the Catholic Monarchs will finance his trip when the war against the Moors has come to an end. The same allegorical figure takes him to talk to *Providencia*, enthroned and flanked by *Idolatría y Religión*. The former will fight against him in the New World, the latter will see to it that he converts the Indians to Catholicism. The action unfolds as predicted, with audience and protagonist equally knowledgeable about what the future holds, thus eliminating conflict and irony.

El conde Fernán González
("Count Ferdinand Gonzalez")

Toward the beginning of this play, the ghost of the hermit Pelayo delivers the following prophecy to the protagonist:

> *al moro Almanzor*
> *vencerás, aunque, admirados*
> *de un prodigio, tus soldados*
> *tendrán recelo y temor.*
> *Muchas hazañas te esperan,*
> *en bien de la fe que adoro,*
> *contra las armas del Moro,*
> *que vuestra quietud alteran.*
> *Reyes vencerás, de quien*
> *preso dos veces serás;*
> *pero de todas saldrás*
> *con honra, dichoso y bien.*
> *Ruégote que de esta casa*
> *te acuerdes en tus victorias.*

(*Acad.* VII, 420a,b)

("You shall conquer Almanzor the Moor, even though your soldiers, astonished by a miracle, will be worried and fearful. You shall do many great deeds for the sake of the faith that I adore. You shall fight the Moors, who so disturb your peace of mind, and you shall conquer kings, whose prisoner you shall twice be; but you shall come out of all these battles with honor, happiness, and success. I beg you to remember this house in all your victories.")

Everything that the hermit Pelayo predicts turns out to be true, but there is no irony here because Fernán González himself is as certain of the future as is the audience or the reader. During Act I he doubts his own omnipotence long enough to ask God for help, but his foreknowledge of his victorious future is reconfirmed by the ghost of Pelayo. A vision of Santiago also appears, and this serves to strengthen his faith. Prophecies of victory and good fortune, then, are not rejected by those to whom they are revealed, so the characters feel no conflict or doubt about what lies ahead. The audience's attention is held not by means of the subtle use of dramatic irony, but rather as a result of various other techniques such as theatrically staged battles, apparitions, disguises, kidnappings and jail breaks to keep the spectators on the edge of their seats. There were also various episodes designed to amuse the audience, such as the appearance of female soldiers or the clever use of the legendary problem of the promissory note which reached astronomical proportions.

It seems evident that the prophecies of clearly "inspired" characters (priests, hermits, national heroes, etc.) invariably turn out to be true, because God is on their side. The taboo against paying credence to prognostications is thereby lifted, for when God wishes to communicate with His creatures it would be wrong *not* to listen. We have seen that in terms of purely dramatic considerations these plays tend to lose a certain efficacy, for the tensions and conflicts that give rise to dramatic irony are necessarily absent.

Los Ramírez de Arellano[68]
("The Ramirez Family from Arellano")

At times, however, a character will flatly refuse to listen to the predictions of even the most saintly of personages, often because of some flaw or weakness in his own nature that prevents him from heeding the advice. Such is the case in the last act of *"Los Ramírez de Arellano,"* when Peter the Cruel makes a passing allusion to the fact that a priest had warned

---

[68] The family name *Arellano* derives from the Late Latin "[fundus] Aurelianus", meaning the farm or estate of the [Roman] Aurelius (now located in Navarre, Spain).

him that his brother was plotting to kill him. Oddly enough Lope misses a good opportunity here to develop the potential irony of the situation, which is described in much greater detail in the Chronicles,[69] where one can find a rather laconic account of the shocking story of how a cleric approached King Pedro (Peter the Cruel) and informed him that Santo Domingo de la Calzada appeared to him in a dream and told him to warn the King that his brother was plotting to kill him. The King was outraged by the news, and asked the cleric if someone had sent him to tell this story. The cleric said no, it was Santo Domingo who gave him the message in a dream. So the King made him tell the story again in front of his courtiers, after which the King was convinced that someone in his court had induced the cleric to relate this message to him, so he ordered him to be burned to death right in front of those who had just heard the cleric's story.

Lope, however, chose not to show the fiery execution on stage, an event that would have been highly dramatic while at the same time graphically revealing the true extent of the

---

[69] Pero López de Ayala, año XI, cap. ix, *Crónica del rey don Pedro,* gives a good account: "Estando el Rey en aquel logar de Azofra, cerca de Nájera, llegó a él un clérigo de misa, que era natural de santo Domingo de la Calzada, e díjole que quería fablar con él aparte: é el Rey díxole que le placia de le oir. E el clérigo le dixo así: 'Señor, Sancto Domingo de la Calzada me vino en sueños, é me dixo que viniese á vos, é que vos dixesse que fuéssedes cierto que si non vos guardásedes, que el Conde D. Enrique vuestro hermano vos avía de matar por sus manos.' E el Rey, desque esto oyó, fué muy espantado, é dixo al clérigo, que si avia alguno que le consejara decir esta razon: é el clérigo dixo que non, salvo Sancto Domingo, que ge le mandara decir. E el Rey mandó llamar á los que y estaban, é mandó al clérigo que dixesse esta rason delante dellos, segund que ge lo avia dicho á él aparte: é el clérigo dixo lo segund que primero lo avia dicho. E el Rey pensó que lo decia por inducimiento de algunos, é mandó luego quemar al clérigo allí do estaba delante de sus tiendas." Quoted by Menéndez Pelayo, *Acad.* IX, clii. (The accentuation and spelling is written according to the *Crónica* cited.)

cruelty of Pedro el Cruel. Be that as it may, the spectators knew the King was to be murdered, so they were well aware of the double irony of his characteristically arrogant belief in his own invulnerability, coupled with the sin of executing a man of God for warning him of his own impending death.

Accurate prophecies, however, are by no means voiced only by priests or angels or allegorical figures. In many cases a true prophecy is made by astrologers, witches, Moors or even the Devil himself,[70] but when properly understood it almost always comes true.[71]

La comedia de Bamba
("The Story of Bamba")

In *La comedia de Bamba,* the Moorish captive Mujarbo predicts that the wicked adviser Ervigio will kill the saintly King Bamba and take the throne for himself. The prophecy is corroborated by an angel who appears to Bamba in a dream and tells him that it is God's will that he should die soon and

---

[70] In *El Arauco domado* the Devil tells Caupolicán that the Spanish will conquer his people, but he nonetheless advises the Indian to fight the invaders, since a victory for them would mean an embarrassing defeat for him (Satan). The Devil, of course, is condemned to struggle eternally against his knowledge of God's will, a fate which makes him a dramatic, if not a heroic, personage. Caupolicán, in choosing to follow the Devil's advice instead of his prophecy, becomes an ironic figure.

[71] There is a student astrologer in *El duque de Viseo* whose prophecy turns out to be untrue: in order to flatter Viseo he tells him that he will be given the throne. This false prediction ironically speeds up the tragic end, for his note falls into the hands of the King, who kills the Duke for being a traitor. The foolish student illustrates a belief commonly accepted in Lope's day and expressed by Mauricio in Book I, xiii of the *Persiles:* "because no science, *qua* science, ever deceives; the deceit lies in the man who does not know the science..." Quoted and translated by Green, *op. cit.,* vol. II, p. 242. We shall see how this belief is incorporated into several of the plays to be examined below.

give the throne to Ervigio. When King Bamba awakens he calls for some water and calmly drinks from the goblet that Ervigio hands him, even though he knows (and we know) that it contains poison. As he dies he announces that Ervigio is to succeed him as King, adding a comment of his own that seems to pass unnoticed by everyone but the audience: *Que siempre una mala obra/ Con otra buena se paga* ["Every bad deed is paid for by another good one" (*Acad.* VII, 72b)].

This ending is relatively unusual in Lope's plays, for ordinarily the wicked are punished and the virtuous are rewarded, but here justice seems to have been suspended. The ironic figure is Ervigio, of course, who mistakenly believes he has deceived the King and won the game, but Bamba's last words are full of double meaning:

> *Ya, fortuna, me has subido*
> *al lugar que deseaba;*
> *tu rueda constante y firme*
> *no ruedes y me deshaga.*   (*Acad.* VII, 72b)

("At last, fortune, you have lifted me up to to the place where I wanted to be; do not spin your firm and faithful wheel and destroy me.")

Everyone knows that Fortune's wheel is anything but firm or faithful, so the day will come when Ervigio will be undone just as he fears. When and how depends on the will of God, the ultimate ironist.

La desdichada Estefanía
("The Sorrowful Stephanie")

I am aware of only one other exception to my statement that prophecies generally turn out to be true in Lope's theatre, and this occurs in *La desdichada Estefanía*. A Moorish soothsayer tells Andelmón:

Rey del África serás,
a España con gente irás;
tu frente espera un laurel,
que en todas las ojas de él
un reino, Andelmón, pondrás.

(*BAE,* XIX, 86a)

("You will be a king of Africa, and you will lead your people to Spain; your head will be crowned with laurels, and you, Andelmón, will build a kingdom on every one of its leaves.")

Although Andelmón does go to Spain, he wins neither laurels nor kingdoms; instead, King Alfonso takes him prisoner and finally sends him back to Africa. No spectator acquainted with the historical facts would have been fooled by the prophecy, so the audience once again sees further than the character. The irony of this play is highly unusual, for Andelmón emerges as an ironic figure who believes a false prophecy, unlike the ironic figures of other plays who refuse to believe true ones.

But prophecies are often misinterpreted by the characters to whom they are revealed, and this becomes an important source of dramatic irony when the audience, from its God-like distance, understands both the truth of the prediction and the deception of the character. We saw how King Rodrigo misread the meaning of his having dropped his crown and scepter, and we were able to smile ironically at the misplaced pride which was at the root of his ignorance.

El piadoso aragonés
("The Pious Aragonese")

A similarly ironic deception occurs in this play when Doña Ana is told by a Moorish soothsayer that Fernando will one day be the King of Aragon. The ambitious lady believes that she will be able to use this foreknowledge to her own advantage by making the young Fernando promise to marry her when he becomes King. But the spectators immediately perceive the irony of this request, for they know that he will only become the King of Aragon *after* he has married Isabel. The Moor has revealed only a portion of the whole truth, so Ana's partial knowledge becomes the focus of irony.

Every member of the audience could easily be expected to know enough history to understand the irony of Rodrigo's false hopes and Doña Ana's mistaken expectations, for the legend of *el último godo* and the reign of Ferdinand and Isabel were known throughout the world. But there are times when one can assume that the accuracy of prophecies (or certain portions of them) must remain a mystery to the audience, since only a fairly specialized knowledge of history would reveal the truth of the prophecy from the start. Such is the case in the play that follows.

La tragedia del rey don Sebastián
("The Tragedy of King Sebastian")

Lela begs the prophetess Celinda to let her see in her mirror the outcome of the struggle for the throne that is being waged between Mahamet, Maluco, and her lover, Hamet. Celinda accedes to her wishes, so Lela looks into the mirror and sees Mahamet drown in a river.[72] She also sees Maluco,

---

[72] The majority of the play's spectators would have been acquainted well enough with the ballads to know that Don Sebastián lost the battle, so the death of Mahamet (his ally as indicated by the play itself) would confirm the accuracy of the prophecy. The spectators' foreknowledge of the Portuguese King's defeat allows them to see the irony inherent in the warnings given to him by his advisers (who remind him that he has no heirs), and by Felipe II (who warns him not to go in person). There is further irony in Sebastián's proud over-confidence, for he takes a crown and scepter to Africa so he will have them on hand when he wins.

who appears to be dead on a stretcher. She assumes, therefore, that Hamet will be King, so she wants to run and tell him the good news. Celinda, however, sternly instructs her to keep her knowledge to herself, warning her that if she tells Hamet anything, she will bring disaster to many people.

But there are few characters in Lope's plays who are able to keep secrets, and Lela is no exception. Soon she tells Hamet that she knows he is to be King. Hamet does not quite believe her, but he allows her to place a crown of flowers on his head. The spectators by this time are no doubt beginning to believe they foresee disaster in store for the unsuspecting Hamet, not only because Lela has broken her promise of secrecy, but also because of the *hubris* (pride) that Hamet showed in wearing his crown of flowers, a sight that enrages Maluco. Shortly afterward the doomed Don Sebastián also angers Maluco by bringing his own crown with him, so we suspect that Hamet and Don Sebastián might share the same fate and that Maluco might prevail, especially since it was not clear that he was really dead on the stretcher in the image that Lela saw.

But just as we begin to strengthen our opinion on these matters, Lope closes the first act with the defeat of Sebastián, Mahamet, and Maluco, so Hamet wins the crown after all. The prediction turns out to be true, but this time the audience was not given enough information to see more clearly than the characters themselves, so although the foreshadowing produces considerable suspense, it is almost devoid of irony. The rest of the play loses dramatic force now that the outcome of the prophecy has been revealed, so Lope demands that we concentrate our attention on Hamet's conversion to Christianity.

Here, then, is a play in which the device of prophecy is used to predict the future correctly, but in spite of the foreshadowing the spectators are unable to view the action from an ironic distance because Lope prefers to keep them in suspense by preventing them from foreseeing the ending. The author is himself the supreme ironist this time, while both the audience and most of the players (except Celinda and Lela) are kept in ignorance.

El Hamete de Toledo
("Hamed of Toledo")[73]

Lope uses a prophecy to surprise the audience in still another way in *El Hamete de Toledo*. The Moorish *hechicera* (witch) Dalima has a book of symbolic representations whose cryptic meanings she interprets in order to foresee the future. She tells Hamete that he will lose his wife Argelina, and she also predicts that he will torture Christian slaves, whose souls will go to heaven. The last prediction was based on her interpretation of a picture that showed human beings nailed to a stake, underneath a group of crosses that were ascending into heaven.

The first part of the prophecy comes true just before the end of Act I: the Christians capture and enslave Hamete and Argelina, who are permanently separated from that time on. The spectators have every reason to believe that the second part of the prophecy will also come true, for Lope carefully establishes Hamete as a sanguine, arrogant character, easily affronted and violent in his desire for revenge. As the play closes he has broken away from captivity and has killed several Christians, but they were not slaves and he did not torture them.

Eventually he is recaptured by the Christians who nail *him* to a stake and torture him. At the very last minute Hamete suddenly claims that he believes in God and asks to be baptized—he has achieved an understanding of his own

---

[73] Hamete is the Spanish version of the Arabic name Hamed, meaning *he who praises.*

destiny through Dalima's symbolic pictures, even though she misinterpreted the meanings. He realizes as he is dying that he himself is the human being nailed to the stake, and the crosses represent his own soul on its way to heaven. Much could be said here about the theological implications of this miracle, but from a dramatic point of view we see once again that Lope was the ironist, while both the audience and the characters in the play were ignorant of the real meaning of the prophecy. What appeared to be clear to the spectators was in reality known only to the author, who ironically used this device of foreshadowing to prevent them from foreseeing the ending as he intended it to be.

On other occasions we have seen that prophecies are misinterpreted by the characters to whom they are revealed, with the result that their ignorance causes them to become ironic figures in the eyes of the audience who, if given sufficient information and not deliberately deceived by the playwright, can naturally see more deeply than the characters. A good Shakespearean example of this kind of irony occurs in *Macbeth,* when the witches tell Macbeth that he will never be vanquished "till Birnam Wood remove to Dunsinane." The audience suspects that the prophecy will come true, but it does not know *how* it will occur. Macbeth is the only one to be lulled into a false sense of security by the belief that the Wood could not possibly move.

El marido más firme
("The Most Steadfast Husband")

In this play, however, ironic ignorance is not so evident in the character to whom the prophecy is revealed as it is to those who interact with her in the play. Eurídice neither deceives herself nor misinterprets the words of Venus, who informs her that her marriage to Orfeo is going to be *breve, gustoso, y perdido* ("brief, enjoyable, and doomed").[74] Even though Eurídice is saddened by this prediction, she believes that she nevertheless has good reason to try to face the truth of the situation:

> *Los sabios, que no se ciegan,*
> *dicen, y han de ser creídos,*
> *que los males prevenidos*
> *son menores cuando llegan.*
> *Pues si yo prevengo el mío*
> *claro está que no será*
> *tan grande llegando ya.*
>
> (*Acad* VI, 179a)

("Wise men, who see all things clearly say, and they have to be believed, that a disaster foreseen is less serious when it finally occurs. So if I foresee my own, it will not, of course, be so bad when it actually happens.")

The very fact that Eurídice tries to mitigate the harshness of the prophecy by facing the truth as she understands it only serves to heighten the irony of her good intentions, for the audience knows (through the myth of Orpheus and Eurydice) that she must eventually die.

But her friend Fílida refuses to agree with her interpretation, preferring to read the oracle's message in a manner which bodes well for the future. She understands *breve* to mean that she will be wed very soon (not that the marriage itself will be brief). As for *perdido*, the optimistic Fílida is certain that this indicates that her husband will be *perdido de amor por ella* (hopelessly in love with her). There is an ironic truth in this apparent misinterpretation, for we know

[74] (*Acad.* VI, 178a).

that Orpheus' love will cause him to lose Eurídice, but in a way that cannot be foreseen by the characters themselves. Fílida's ignorance of the real meaning of the oracle, then, causes her to be an ironic figure, for the audience sees the uselessness of her carefree optimism. To the extent that Eurídice is unaware of the nature of her destiny she, too, is an ironic figure, but she acquires a tragic dimension in her foreknowledge of doom and in her willingness to face it. She even tries actively to avoid doing anything which could hasten the progress of the oracle's prediction, so she flees from Aristeo when he declares his love for her, ironically hoping to escape thereby the unhappiness that nevertheless must sooner or later overtake her. But she cannot retain this tenuous control over her destiny for very long. She, like the passionate lovers to be discussed in Part Three, will soon surrender to Don Amor.

The young women finally decide to pay a visit to Orfeo (Orpheus), who is reputed to be an excellent interpreter of the mysterious prophecies of Venus. Before they arrive, Lope presents Orfeo cleverly explaining various oracles to some shepherds who have come to him for advice. But no sooner does he lay eyes on Eurídice than he falls in love with her, and love's blindness promptly causes him to lose his powers of divination, for when questioned about the meaning of the prophecy of Venus, he ironically agrees with Fílida's false interpretation (*Acad* VI, 183b), adding that he himself is surely the husband that Venus had in mind.[75] Fabio is astonished at Orfeo's sudden decision to marry Eurídice:

---

[75] This is ironically the only true part of his interpretation. There is so much verbal irony in these verses that it would be impossible to cover it all; one of the most prophetic statements, however, is Orfeo's promise: "Seré tuya hasta la muerte" ("I shall be yours till death do us part.") (183b).

Tú, para todas cruel
¿aquí tan blando? No creo
que nace de tu deseo;
veneno te han dado en él;
Venus airada, el Amor,
su hijo, se han conjurado
contra ti, que has despreciado
su poder y su valor.

(*Acad* VI, 184a)

("You who are so cruel to the gentle sex, what softens you
now? I do not believe that it springs from your desire. Proud
Venus, along with Love, her son, have poisoned your heart
and conspired against you because you looked down on their
power and their bravery.")

Lope is using a classical theme that has tragic potential:
the Greek gods often punished mortals for being too aloof
by pushing them into passionate affairs whose outcome was
inevitably disastrous. But when Fabio warns Orfeo about the
danger that he is courting, Orfeo pays no attention at all to
his warning, telling him that if the gods have decided to give
Eurídice to him, what's wrong with that? ("Fabio, si a Eurídice bella/ me dan, ¿qué llamas agravio?" *Acad* VI, 184a)

It is Eurídice who turns out to be the tragic figure, for
although her will is overpowered by the passion she feels for
Orfeo, she nonetheless has a strong foreboding about the outcome of their upcoming nuptials. She is also deeply troubled
by the bad omen that takes place at their wedding: her portrait mysteriously falls down and then jumps magically back
into place.[76] Shortly before she is bitten by the asp she loses
a portrait of Orfeo, an omen whose obvious meaning is not

[76] In Ovid's account the wedding is also plagued by bad omens. See the
Metamorphoses, X, 4-7.

lost on her. She cannot hide from herself the foreknowledge of her infelicitous destiny, yet at the same time her passion prevents her from wishing that it could be otherwise. With the death of the tragic heroine the play loses its force, not out of dramatic necessity (Orfeo's journey to the underworld and his second loss of Eurídice has tragic potential) but because Lope could not resist the temptation of making the *gracioso* Fabio into a farcical figure whose comments on the denizens of Hades (after the manner of the *Danza de la muerte*) turn the last act into a comical satire. The subplot presents various problems which have to be resolved in the end through the customary marriages, and Orfeo more or less gets lost in the shuffle. Lope was not unaware of the inconclusiveness of his play (which is by no means a tragedy), for he promises the audience a second part which he never wrote.

The plays that we have just discussed offer examples of dramatic irony that varies according to the degree of awareness which develops in the characters as a result of the information given to them through the prophecies. We have seen that the characters whose foreknowledge is nearly perfect (*Los trabajos de Jacob*) lack the ironic dimension of those who are fooled by their own self-deception or misinterpretations (*El último godo*), for the latter are ignorant of their own destinies, and consequently the audience, knowing more than they do, can view their futile actions from an ironic distance. We have also seen that those characters who are clearly villains (*El bastardo Mudarra*) or innocent victims (*El marqués de Mantua*) are not tragic heroes no matter how aware they may be of what awaits them, for the former are too evil to represent the classical "noble figure with a tragic flaw," while the latter are simply too passive to struggle heroically against a destiny they dimly foresee but cannot or will not attempt to modify. Lope's characters are not always at the mercy of a foreseeable destiny, however, for once in a while they ignore the predictions suggested by the foreshadowing,

and they bravely confront the events that are supposedly predestined to occur. The plays that illustrate the determined
attitude and courageous actions of this type of hero will now
be examined in Part Two.

PART TWO

The Triumph of Free Will

The theological implications of the perennial question of free will and determinism gave rise to many discussions and treatises in the Golden Age,[77] and the popular theme was naturally reflected in the *Comedia,* especially in the plays of Tirso de Molina and Calderón de la Barca. Although Lope does not delve quite as deeply as his two successors into the complex problems that are raised by these issues, he is still concerned with the questions of man's destiny and the extent to which he may or may not control it. In Part Three we shall examine a number of plays in which it becomes evident that the one force that can most successfully overcome man's free will is amorous passion. Although the stars cannot force the free will to love, a man or woman, once in love, is almost incapable of renouncing passion, and thus it would seem that a power much stronger than they (such as the stars or destiny) were forcing them to succumb to an irresistible emotion. These doomed lovers who were aware of the danger and yet knew they were powerless to

---

[77] The questions were discussed for centuries by Catholic theologians, but they were raised again by the Protestants, which prompted new polemics during the Counter-Reformation in Spain. The Dominican Domingo Báñez, who sought to limit the power of free will in his doctrine of "premonición física," was strongly opposed by the Jesuit Luis de Molina, who defended free will in his *Concordia liberi arbitrii cum gratiae donis* ("The Harmony of Free Will with Gifts of Grace").

avoid it turned out to be tragic figures, tragic because they were responsible for their fate and yet victimized by their passion. They were also ironic figures to the audience, who contemplated their false hopes and self-deception from the distance of one who knows better. Their inner struggle, then, was the basis for the conflict presented on the stage.

But Lope occasionally dramatized a different struggle, one that was neither tragic nor ironic, nor fought within the character himself; instead, the hero pitted his strength against destiny itself, and if he was a noble, virtuous man, he would always emerge triumphant. A speech from *El animal profeta* serves as an illustration:

> *Dios ha dado a los hombres*
> *libre albedrío, y con éste*
> *deben los cuerdos varones*
> *prevenirse a las desdichas*
> *y resistir a sus golpes.*

("God gave men free will, and with this gift sensible men should foresee misfortune and resist its blows.")

Contra valor no hay desdicha
("Courage Never Brings Misfortune")

Perhaps the best example of this popular theme can be found in *Contra valor no hay desdicha*, a play we discussed previously from another angle (p. 40) and which was written in Lope's later years (1625?-1630?). The plot is based on a well-known story: Ciro (Cyrus), a handsome young *aldeano* (villager), sees himself as the "king" of the countryside. He soon wins such fame for his courage and qualities of leadership that he is brought to the attention of the real King. As soon as the King lays eyes on the youth he recognizes him to be his own grandson, a fact that causes him great anguish because he had once been told by some astrologers that the newborn child would some day take the throne. The King had ordered his adviser to throw him secretly to the wild beasts in the forest, but the adviser disobeyed the order and gave the baby to a peasant to raise as her own. At this point various types of foreshadowing come into play: when Ciro's identity is revealed the King foresees that the boy will be a danger to him, for he already shows every sign of being a strong opponent. Ciro's foster father fears that the boy's sense of leadership and self-confidence will get him into trouble, and the adviser fears that his strong, independent spirit will somehow cause a disaster. The King, however, temporarily tricks everybody into believing that he is wise and benevolent by pretending to welcome Ciro to the palace and asking the adviser to tutor the boy in the art of courtesy. But if the audience or the characters are at first taken in by this deception, they soon learn that the King's villainous character has not changed, for he not only orders some soldiers to ambush Ciro and kill him, but he even serves the adviser his own son on a platter at the dinner table as punishment for his insubordination.

Although the King enjoys the role of *eirōn*[78] during the time he deceives his subjects with his false benevolence, the tables are soon turned on him and he becomes the *alazōn* (the ironic dupe) of a larger design that he is spiritually unprepared to understand. Ciro easily overcomes the soldiers' incompetent attempt on his life, and he joins forces with the outraged adviser against the King, saying that it is madness for his grandfather to try to oppose the divine decree which had been revealed to him by the astrologers.

---

[78] The Greeks applied this term to certain characters who, like Socrates, could see through the ignorant pose of an *alazōn (dupe or fool)* and deftly expose him by the use of ironic argument.

From now on the evil and ironic figure of the King will
be juxtaposed with the virtuous Ciro who usurps the role of
eirōn from him, for he is graced with a superior knowledge
of the heavenly decree and can thus foresee the outcome of
the ensuing action. He sends a messenger to tell the King
that he intends to attack him with his army of followers
because he has shown himself to be an unjust ruler and also
because the kingdom rightly belongs to him. He warns the
King not to resist him, for heaven is on his side. But Lope is
not willing to let the spectators be too complacent in the
foreknowledge they now believe they share with Ciro, for he
presents them with all sorts of prodigies and evil omens
concerning the hero and his men: his horse falls down, the
sombra of his real father warns him not to attack, and a
comet flies across the sky.

The soldiers and the foster father are terrified by these
ominous prodigies, but Ciro remains unperturbed. He kills
his horse to prove to his men that even the stars themselves
have no influence over a virtuous man who puts his faith in
God, and with that he marches off to fight the King's troops.
During the battle it is made clear that God is indeed on his
side, for he is miraculously invulnerable to the arrows that
hit him from all sides. When the King sees this he throws
himself at Ciro's feet and begs him for mercy, declaring that
he now realizes that he was mad to have gone against the
decree of heaven. Ciro pardons him and then magnanimously
gives him an important city to rule, but he takes for himself
the crown to which he is entitled, thus fulfilling the prophecy
of the astrologer and illustrating the belief that man can
overcome the ascendancy of the stars, but he cannot, and
ought not, challenge the will of God.[79]

---

[79] The stars may incline a man's will for good or for evil, but they do not
determine his actions. Man alone is responsible for these, but his virtue
depends on his confidence in God's will and his ability to love Him and

Lo que está determinado
("What Has Been Determined")

There is a slight variation in the ending of this earlier play, (1613-1619) which is otherwise almost exactly like the one that has just been discussed. In that play the grandson enters the palace with his men, only to find the King cowering in the corner of the patio, unconvincingly disguised as a gardener. This time the grandson not only forgives him for all his crimes, but he assures him that he has no intention of depriving him of the throne—he only wants to establish the fact that he is the rightful heir. The King is so moved by his grandson's charity that he gives him the kingdom of his own free will, thus ironically fulfilling the prophecy that he had fought so hard to suppress.

There is one other aspect of the problem of free will and determinism that is brought out quite clearly in both plays, and this involves the questions that are inevitably raised by Lope's treatment of the theme of love. To what extent is love determined by outside factors, and how much does it depend on free will? There is often a crucial element involved in the lover's choice of a loved-one, a choice that is not always left entirely to chance. This element, as Lope sees it, is a sort of sensitivity felt and shared by the highly-born who recognize in each other a certain nobility of feeling and spiritual depth which cannot exist in the coarser natures of the "lowly."[80]

---

his neighbours more than himself. This doctrine is midway between "impecabilidad" and fatalism, but there is no room here even to begin to approach an adequate documentation of the sources. For an excellent bibliography and discussion of the many aspects of these problems, see Marcel Bataillon, *Erasme et l'Espagne,* Paris, 1937.

[80] José F. Montesinos has examined the character of this inherited quality in his introduction to *El cuerdo loco* ("The Sane Madman"), *TAE,* IV, 185, and also in the study that accompanies *La corona merecida* ("The Merited Crown") *TAE,* V, 155 ff. The following comments, taken from his article "Algunas observaciones sobre la figura del donaire en *Lope de*

For this reason Ciro (*Contra valor no hay desdicha*) loves
Fílis, a lady of the court, even though he himself is thought
to be a humble peasant. Appearances deceive, however, and
Ciro is driven by the promptings of his inner nobility to
follow his lofty aspirations, much to the horror of his companions, who foresee nothing but pain and disaster as a result
of what to them is inexplicable behavior. But Ciro, seeing
more deeply than they do, is completely undisturbed by their
predictions of doom, so this time it is the warning figures
themselves (rather than the character who refuses to heed the
warning) who become the ironic dupes of a reality they can
not be expected to understand.

Love, then, begins as an act of recognition, but it is also
subject to the influence of other factors. In the first scene of
Lo que está determinado, Carlos tries to compel Rosaura to
love him by threatening her with the regal power he acquired
when he was crowned "king" by his companions, but he is
met with coy refusal:

Rosaura: *Amor no se ha de mandar*
porque es amor influencia

Vega," Salamanca (Anaya) 1967, p.23, apply very well to the two plays
presently under discussion: "Nobleza es un concepto que se predica del
alma y de la estirpe; es anhelo y hazaña y alienta en el espíritu a la vez
como aspiración, esfuerzo y conciencia. Nobleza es la sensibilidad para
la aventura y el valor personal; nobleza que el caballero afirma con una
alta conciencia de sí mismo. Pero es la sangre heredada la que determina
la trayectoria de la voluntad. La sangre heredada hace al héroe serlo.
Podrá éste encontrarse en las circunstancias más desfavorables, des-
conocido, apartado del mundo; podrá desconocer él mismo la alteza de su
condición; no importa. El más leve rumor de guerra hará que el arco de
su voluntad se dispare; será diestro en la batalla, ordenará las haces según
una refinada ciencia no aprendida. Es la sangre… El amor encontrará en
él una sensibilidad más despierta que la de ningún otro, porque la sensibilidad para el amor es un atributo de la nobleza, y ese amor tenderá a
nobles objetos."

> *de las estrellas.*
> Carlos: *Los sabios*
> *mandan también las estrellas.*
> *Yo mando a las de tus ojos*
> *que me quieran.*   (*Acad.* VII, 223b)

("*Rosaura:* Love should not be forced, because love is influenced by the stars. *Carlos:* Wise men also command the stars. I order the stars in your eyes to love me.")

Love indeed cannot be forced, but if the rules of courtship are properly observed and understood, it can often be coaxed. Thus Carlos pretends to be interested in another *aldeana* (villager) to arouse Rosaura's jealousy, but she feels very angry with him, of course, and claims to be thoroughly unimpressed by this feint. But when it seems as if their love might be made impossible by the discovery of his royal heritage, then her passion is greatly increased. Neither man nor star can force free will to love but, in Lope's opinion, the stars can incline the lovers' will, and obstacles can usually be trusted to crystallize the growing passion. When this happens free will is subordinated to the demands of love, whether they be constructive, as in the case of Carlos and Rosaura (whose love is eventually fulfilled), or destructive, as in the case of tragic passion.[81]

---

[81] Juan B. Avalle-Arce, in *La novela pastoril española,* Madrid, 1959, p. 137, notes that "La gran afición de Lope a las artes mágicas y afines está bien estudiada en el artículo de Juan Millé y Giménez, 'El horóscopo de Lope de Vega,' *Humanidades,* XV (1927), 69-96. According to Avalle-Arce, Millé points out that even if the lovers' stars are so disposed as to make them fall fatally in love, there are still ways of curing passion: time and the application of various remedies (first suggested by Ovid and elaborated by Ficino) will cure love despite the influence of the stars, as seen, for example, in *La Dorotea.* Lope is neither a 'credulous charlatan' nor is he completely dominated by a belief in irremediable predestination in matters of love, but there is no doubt that he 'showed a very marked

Lo que ha de ser
("What is Meant to Be")

It is appropriate to close this section with a discussion of *Lo que ha de ser,* for it unites and dramatizes most of the main topics that have been studied so far. The foreshadowing in this play is well established from the beginning: an astrologer once told the King that his son would be killed by a lion before his fourteenth birthday. The King tries to prevent the fulfillment of this prophecy by locking up the boy in a castle so that no lion might ever come within reach of him.

The Prince's reaction to his imprisonment is not unlike Segismundo's;[82] his unnatural confinement inevitably makes him brutal, self-centered and violent, despite his tutor's efforts to teach him virtue. One day he falls in love with Laura (a noble lady disguised as a peasant) who comes to entertain him at the castle, and he demands to be allowed to go to the village to see her. The King refuses, but he orders his men to kidnap her and bring her to the castle.

The Prince is warned to control his desire ("vencer tu propia pasión/ fué siempre el mayor trofeo" ("the ability to conquer your own desire was always the greatest trophy," *Acad* XII, p. 393a), but he pays no attention to the advice, insisting instead that his passion has now freed him from the hated prophecy, for Laura has Leo rising on her birth chart and she has "killed" him with her amorous passion. Now that the prophecy has supposedly been fulfilled, the Prince sees no reason why he should not leave the castle, but the King is unconvinced by his argument and he forces him to remain a prisoner.

---

interest in astrology,' and treated it, 'entre burlas y veras' in many of his works throughout his life" (Millé, p. 69).

[82] This play might be added to the list of sources of *La vida es sueño.* Arturo Farinelli (*La vita é un sogno,* 2 vols., Turin, 1929) does not mention it in his extensive examination of the sources of Calderón's play.

The Prince turns his attention to his hostage and orders her to love him. When he finds she cannot obey him he tries to rape her, but he is frustrated by the intervention of the tutor. Shortly afterward Leonardo, a peasant from the village, goes to the castle to rescue Laura. The tutor tells Leonardo that he is the illegitimate son of the King, but that he had been abandoned in the village long ago because the King thought the lion of the prophecy referred to him. The tutor then suggests that he kill his half brother and seize the throne (the tutor is tired of tending to the petulant Prince), not only because the crown is his birthright but also because the stars have decreed it. But Leonardo is incorruptible:

> *El que es fuerte*
> *es señor de las estrellas,*
> *aunque me lo manden ellas*
> *puedo yo con mi albedrío*
> *gozar de mi señorío*
> *y dejar de obedecellas.*
> *Por lo que tienen poder*
> *es por la flaqueza humana,*
> *que hace resistencia llana*
> *a lo que quiere hacer.*
> *Yo no tengo de poner*
> *mano en mi sangre, Severo;*
> *morir a las suyas quiero;*
> *busque el cielo otro león,*
> *si es que importa a su opinión*
> *salir con tan mal agüero.*
>
> (*Acad.* N. XII, 399b-400a)

("The strong man is lord of the stars, so even if they try to dominate me I can use my free will to enjoy my authority and refuse to obey them. They [the stars] are only powerful when it comes to human weakness, which offers naught but ignoble resistence to what it wants to do. I have no need to lift my hand against my own relatives, Severo; I want to die by *their* hands; let the heavens look for another lion, if it matters so much to them to be ruled by such an evil omen.")

When the Prince discovers that Laura is really a princess, he decides to marry her regardless of her feelings. He is so exultant at having thus conquered the "lion" that he orders an artist to paint a portrait of him standing with one foot resting triumphantly on the body of a dead lion. The painting is duly executed and placed on a piece of furniture that happens to be directly in front of some swords that decorate the wall. As the Prince contemplates the painting he is suddenly seized by a feeling of uncontrollable rage toward the lion that had kept him locked up for so long, so he puts his fist right through the canvas, mortally wounding himself on the swords that are mounted on the wall behind the painting. The King, realizing the prophecy has finally come true, understands at last the futility of all his attempts to change heaven's decree:

> *¡Cielos, qué sucesos tales!*
> *¡Ay, Albano, que ahora veo*
> *que nuestras fuerzas notables*
> *no impiden lo que ha de ser,*
> *que es el cielo investigable!*

> * * * *

> *Siempre fué lo que ha de ser*
> *por más que el hombre se guarde.*
> (*Acad.* N. XII, 405b-406a)

("Heavens, what extraordinary goings on! Oh, Albano [the tutor], I see now that even by our best efforts we cannot stop what is meant to be, for heaven will not be challenged. *What is meant to be* has always prevailed, no matter what men try to do to protect themselves from it.")

A comparison of the speeches of Leonardo and the King would seem to indicate a philosophical contradiction in their positions, for while Leonardo declares that the strong man is lord of the stars, the King maintains that man's best efforts cannot prevail against what is meant to be. When examined in the context of the whole play, however, these statements both prove to be true, for the noble, virtuous man can master the influence of the stars by controlling his impulses and acting ethically under all circumstances; but the willful, self-centered, ignoble individual is destined to fail no matter how hard he tries to change the decree of the heavens, for God's will cannot be challenged. It is important to distinguish between the meaning of *the stars* and *what is meant to be;* the one indicating a force that can influence us for good or for evil depending on our personal inclinations, and the other being a way of describing God's will for our lives, which cannot be changed by mortal fiat.

Lope's play is well conceived and beautifully balanced in that it presents two ways of reacting to the "stars" and two ways of confronting "what is meant to be." The Prince quickly succumbs to what he considers to be the influence of the stars, and surrenders himself completely to his passionate desire for Laura. Leonardo, on the other hand, is not moved by ambition or greed, and refuses to kill his half brother, even if the stars should try to influence him to do so. As for "what is meant to be," the King tries his best to challenge fate by imposing his will on other people and depriving them of their freedom, with disastrous results. Leonardo, on the other hand, does not meddle with people's lives, nor does he try to serve his own interests at the expense of others; he even goes so far as to give up Laura to the Prince rather than resort to criminal means to prevent their union:

> *Goce a Laura, aunque la adoro,*
> *y goce el reino mi hermano.*

> (*Acad.* N. XII, 400a)

("Let him enjoy Laura, even though I adore her, and may my
brother enjoy the kingdom.")

When seen from a purely dramatic point of view, the
prophecy and the reaction of the characters afford material
for ironic situations. The way in which the prophecy was to
be fulfilled is typically misinterpreted by the King and the
Prince, but this time the spectators are also kept in the dark,
for they cannot foresee just how the prediction will finally
turn out to be true. But the central irony of the play lies in the
fact that both the Prince and the King become the victims of
the very fate they are trying to avoid, and to a large extent
they themselves are ironically responsible for its fulfillment.
By locking up his son, the King seeks to protect him from an
unhappy fate, but he inadvertently becomes instrumental in
its execution; by locking up the woman he loves, the Prince
thinks he will be able to force her to return his love, but he
succeeds only in making her hate him. Appearances almost
invariably deceive: the castle that appears to be strong and
invulnerable offers no protection to its prisoner; the young
man who is deemed to be a potential murderer turns out to be
more virtuous than those who fear him; the painting that de-
picts the Prince's triumph ironically causes his death.

In this section we have discussed briefly the question of
free will and determinism in three of Lope's plays, and we
mentioned some of the ways in which lovers dealt with the
problems inherent in the conflicting demands of passion.
Men and women can overcome the influence of the stars by
firmly exercising their will to control them, but the outcome
of the struggle is never predictable and it is by no means
easy for the lovers to prevail. In Part Three we shall examine
some of the ironic and tragic results of this struggle on the
part of the characters to deal with the paradoxes of passion.

PART THREE

Passion and Foreshadowing

Perhaps the most dramatic type of foreshadowing to occur in Lope's plays has to do with those portents that are used to warn a lover of the dangers inherent in his ill-advised passion, for in many of the more serious plays this *locura amorosa* ("amorous madness") is responsible for leading him to his own destruction.[83] That passion, in its extreme form, must end in death is borne out by countless examples throughout literature, both ancient and modern. Romeo and Juliet, Pyramus and Thisbe, Tristan and Iseult, Calixto and Melibea—the list is interminable, and so are the theories that attempt to explain this paradox by either attacking or defending the spirit of *erōs*.

Christian moralists generally viewed amorous passion as an example of human weakness and as a temptation that prevents man from loving God and finding spiritual fulfillment. The Romantics, on the other hand, often praised passionate lovers for choosing to live an intense and brief life rather than a long and sensible one.[84] The Freudian school analyzed

---

[83] Much has been written about the origins and history of the traditions of love that make up the basis of our modern notion of "amorous passion." For an excellent bibliography on this subject, see Otis Green, *Spain and the Western Tradition,* Madison (Univ. of Wisconsin Press), 1966, vol. I, pp. 303-317. Particularly pertinent are C.S. Lewis, *The Allegory of Love,* Oxford, 1936; Denis de Rougemont, *L'Amour et l'Occident,* Paris, 1939; and Martin C. D'Arcy, *The Mind and Heart of Love,* London, 1945; and, of course, Andreas Capellanus.

[84] Even later, a Neo-Romantic like Nietzsche, for example, champions passion over commone sense: "There are some who, from obtuseness or

the paradox of love and destruction in terms of the *death wish*, the desire for ultimate union not only with the beloved but with all of nature.[85] De Rougemont speaks of death as the most perfect obstacle to which the lovers must finally resort in order to keep their passion alive.[86] Green points out that life is meaningless for the lover who no longer loves, so death would be preferable to an empty existence.[87] Later on he says that death can also come as a relief to a lover tired of waging an eternal battle within himself.[88] Whatever the reasons for the paradoxes of love and its connection with death, the fact remains that the *sic* (yes) and *non* (no) are always there, and the dilemma experienced by the lover provides ample material for dramatic conflict.

Not all the lovers created by Lope de Vega and his contemporaries, however, were fated to come to such bad ends. Many Golden Age lovers, both young and old, were either too wise or simply too much in control of their emotions to let themselves be carried away by amorous passion. Juan Ruiz de Alarcón, in *No hay mal que por bien no venga* (literally "Every bad situation has its good side," or "Every cloud has a silver lining,"), came up with one of the most engaging, likable midle-aged lovers of seventeenth-century

---

lack of experience, turn away from such phenomena (the dances of St. John and St. Vitus) as from *folk diseases,* with contempt and pity born of the consciousness of their own 'healthy-mindedness.' But of course such poor wretches have no idea how corpse-like and ghostly their so-called 'healthy-mindedness' looks when the glowing life of Dionysian revelers roars past them." Nietzsche, *The Birth of Tragedy,* translation by Walter Kaufmann, N.Y. (Vintage) 1967, pp. 36-37. It should be noted, however, that the last pages of the book show his "wise Athenian" worshipping at the temples of both Apollo and Dionysius (p. 144).

[85] See Sigmund Freud, *Beyond the Pleasure Principle* (1920), *Standard Edition,* London (Hogarth Press), 1955.

[86] Denis de Rougemont, *op. cit.,* see chapter called "The Love of Death."

[87] Otis Green, *op. cit.,* p. 106.

[88] Green, *op. cit.,* p. 152, n. 97.

Spain when he created the character of Don Domingo de Don Blas. This wise and relentlessly honest man refused to deceive himself on any grounds; he refrained from wearing the uncomfortable but fashionable apparel of the day, he firmly renounced the material benefits offered him by a dishonest King, and he unbegrudgingly gave up the woman he loved to the man she herself preferred, in spite of what he would have liked to believe about her inclinations.

The majority of lovers in the Golden Age *Comedia*, however, were certainly vulnerable to passion, and yet they still managed to get married and "live happily ever after." They, too, were susceptible to the pleasurable pain of erotic desire, the overwhelming power of their lady's beauty, and the frustration of her unobtainability. They knew by heart the symptoms of the passion sickness, they all complained of being victimized, enslaved, spurned, and mistreated, yet they kept on serving, suffering, idealizing, and waiting for some sign of mercy from their heartless lady. They were, in short, lovers who represented aspects of many literary traditions as well as being creatures of their author's own imagination.

The passionate love experienced by these charismatic Golden Age characters, however, did not necessarily turn them into tragic figures. This is because the lovers, whether they realized it or not, made a game of the swain/damsel relationship. They knew the rules, and they followed them to the letter because it gave them the desired results: after an exhausting comedy of hide and seek, will she or won't she, does he or doesn't he—the two lovers effectively managed to excite each other's desire to the point where it was no longer bearable, and then the happy declarations were made.

At this stage in the game the lovers were willing to re-linquish their roles because the goal had been achieved, and so the play ended with marriage and merry-making. Their matrimonial future, predictably, was rarely examined by the playwright, for the entertainment value of the exciting stages of passionate love is naturally greater than what can be ex-

pected from the humdrum problems of everyday life.[89] Even
so, we must assume that the lovers considered themselves
fortunate to have brought their affairs to a happy conclusion,
and if they suspected, even dimly, that marriage might cause
the death of passion,[90] we must also assume that they would
somehow make the necessary adjustments and go on from
there to explore different forms of love. Their continued
happiness, then, would have to depend on their ability to
give up the game of passion.

Many of the lovers who concern us in this section, however, were either unwilling or unable to come to terms with
this fact. Each took the game of passion absolutely seriously,
each strove to make his passion endure, each made passion
an end in itself instead of a means to an end. But passion is
full of contradictions, so the lovers encountered their fair
share of insoluble conflicts: passion takes more delight in the
absence than in the presence of the beloved, it becomes
stronger through separation than through union, it dies with
satisfaction but grows as long as the beloved is unattainable,
it needs hope but shuns certainty, it wounds yet refuses all
cures. The paradoxes of passion, then, have been used to
good advantage by Lope in establishing dramatic conflict in
his characters, a conflict heightened by the awareness that
they acquire through the various devices of foreshadowing.

---

[89] A notable exception would be Lope's *La bella malmaridada* (before
1598) in which the married *dama* resorts to coquetry with another *galán*
in order to win back her roving mate. But arousing his passion again by
making him jealous is really only another variation on the old rules of the
game of passion itself.

[90] Some of these lovers were more than a little suspicious of marriage as
a dampener of passion. In *El príncipe perfecto, I,* Don Juan says of Doña
Leonor, who wants to marry him: "¿Qué haré para que Leonor/ No pro-
siga con su intento?/ Pues comienza el casamiento/ Donde se acaba el
amor." (*Acad.* X, 474b). ("What can I do to dissuade Leonor from going
ahead with her plans? For love ends where marriage begins.")

Passion punished: *El robo de Dina*
("The Rape of Dinah")

Awareness can be a deceptive term in many cases, for it becomes necessary to distinguish between superficial awareness based on a familiarity with traditional wisdom, and true self-knowledge which emerges as the result of experience. The trajectory of any well-made play will often lead the protagonist from apparent knowledge to a more substantial, or real knowledge of himself and his circumstances, but Lope did not generally dwell on the classical moment of final recognition. Instead, he preferred to underscore the irony of the character's initial ignorance by providing him with comments that foreshadowed the future action, the significance of which was understood by the audience but not by the character himself.

In the first act of *El robo de Dina,* Siquén's attitude tells us that he is too clever to get trapped by the "come hither glances" of a scheming woman. His comments are ironic not only because his ignorance of his fate is clearly evident to any member of the audience familiar with the Biblical tale,[91] but also because his proud confidence in his invulnerability to passion immediately suggests that he will soon become its victim himself.[92] His boast is a clear foreshadowing of what

---

[91] Genesis:34 describes how Prince Shechem raped Dinah, the daughter of Jacob, and how he then loved her and wished to marry her. The sons of Jacob agreed to the marriage providing Shechem and all the men of the city allowed themselves to be circumcised. Shechem and his men assented, but shortly after the operation Jacob's sons took advantage of their temporary disability to slay them all.

[92] This idea has its roots in classical antiquity, for the gods, particularly Venus, tended to punish those who insulted them by spurning love. One good example in many is Aphrodite's speech in the prologue to *Hippolytus,* when she declares that she will take revenge on the proud young man who is more interested in the hunt than in the pursuit of women. Also interwoven into this situation is the theme of "pride before the fall."

is in store for him, but he is himself completely unaware of how prophetic his words really are, for he has only second-hand knowledge of the destructive power of passion. He feels dangerously confident about his own low opinion of passionate love, boasting that he would far rather spend his time hunting than persuing deceptive illusions.

The gods must have taken note of his youthful *hubris,* however, for no sooner does he lay eyes on Dina than he falls head over heels for her. He knows nothing of the rules of the game, however, for he impetuously declares himself to Dina, who turns him down without a second thought, telling him that his sudden passion is merely an invention of his imagination. She tells him he must prove the authenticity of his love by *porfía* (determination) and the passage of time, for only then will he be able to perceive the real nature of his desire. But Siquén insists that he already knows that his love is genuine, so from this point on he becomes an ironic figure, seeing only what appears to promise bliss and fulfillment, blind to the reality of his unshared excitement, and deaf to Dina's wise admonitions. After being raped by Siquén, she delivers a prophetic warning:

> *Muchos como tú se fían*
> *En los padres que los aman,*
> *Y en las repúblicas tienen*
> *Las dignidades más altas.*
> *Mas sucede que una noche*
> *(Sin que se sepa), la espada,*
> *Atravesada, les tiñe*
> *De sangre y dolor las canas.*
>
> (*Acad*.III, 222b)

("Many men like you depend on the parents who love them, and they enjoy the highest dignity conferred upon them by their republics. But then one night [without anyone's knowing it] the sword slices through them and tinges their white hair with blood and pain.")

The spectators alone understand the true meaning of Dina's words, so now they can watch from an ironic distance as Siquén moves closer and closer to death. As for Siquén him-self, he seems to be totally unaware of any possibility of disenchantment, even though his confidant Alfeo repeatedly warns him of the ironic conflict between appearance and reality when it comes to matters of love. Alfeo reflects the point of view of the practical, down-to-earth *gracioso* or servant who sees only the disadvantages that the fulfillment of purely sexual desire implies: satisfaction kills lust, and ultimately brings pain and repentance.

But Siquén understands nothing of these commonplaces, for like a typical nobleman or *galán,* he has already idealized his lady to such an extent that Alfeo's practical reality cannot penetrate Siquén's imagination. He sees Dina as the embodiment of all beauty, and his love as nothing less than eternal. When he tells Alfeo that he wants to marry her, the confidant once again protests:

> *La abundancia del bien enfadar suele,*
> *y desta hay grande copia en los casados.*
>
> (*Acad.* III, 228a)

("The surfeit of joy tends to irritate, and there is much proof of this in married couples.")

The future as it appears to Siquén through his rose-coloured glasses is in ironic contrast to the future as Alfeo sees it on the template of common sense, a template shared by the spectators as a result of the foreshadowing backed up by the well-known Bible story. But if Siquén's blindness can survive the advice and admonitions offered him by fellow mortals, it cannot remain insensitive to the apparition of a silent *sombra* that suddenly manifests itself before him as he is about to enter Dina's rooms. Unlike the self-possessed and guiltless king in *El príncipe perfecto,* Siquén is terrified of this vision, which he takes to be a portent of doom. He now begins to experience an awareness of his own guilt, for the ghost seems to be trying to prevent him from forcing Dina once more to comply with him against her will.

It is interesting to note that he interprets the *sombra* as being a manifestation of himself, a sort of intuitive creation of a recriminatory superego which unexpectedly takes on a visible form. In this clairvoyant soliloquy he foresees his death, and realizes that it is to come as a result of his own wrong actions. When he tells Alfeo about the specter and the forebodings he feels, Alfeo scoffs at him in much the same way as the friends of other characters who were perturbed by bad omens:

> Alfeo: *¿Tu sombra? ¿Cómo podía…*
> Siquén: *De mi temor fabricada,*
> *la vi con daga y espada.*
> Alfeo: *Todo ha sido fantasía*
> *y vana imaginación:*
> *Ven donde tu padre está.*
> (*Acad.* III, 232b)

> Alfeo: Your shadow? How could it…
> Siquén: It was fashioned out of my fear,
> I saw it with a dagger and a sword.
> Alfeo: It was just fantasy
> and pointless speculation.
> Let us go and see your father.

But Siquén knows better, and now he sees more clearly than his sensible confidant, for he is no longer blind to the destructive nature of his passion:

Siquén: *Notable pena me da;*
      Sombra de mi muerte son.
      ¡Plega a Dios que yo no acierte!
      Porque bien saben los sabios
      que el cuerpo de los agravios
      hace sombras en la muerte!

                                    (*Acad.* III 232b)

Siquén: It gives me great pain;
         They are the shadows of my death.
         Pray God that I am not right!
         For wise men know
         that the sum total of our offences
         become shadows in the hereafter!

His forebodings of doom, however, should not be confused with the audience's certainty of his death;[93] he still is an ironic figure who is essentially ignorant of the real nature of his destiny ("¡Plega a Dios que yo no acierte!"), but his foreboding adds dramatic impact to his situation as well as creating, for the first time, conflict within himself.

It has been mentioned previously that a character is ironic to the extent that he is unaware of his predicament, and tragic to the extent that he is aware of what lies ahead, yet unable or unwilling to do anything to avert the disaster. Although Siquén's self-awareness gives him the potential to be a tragic character, he still cannot develop into a truly tragic figure, partly because the rape of Dina prevents him from eliciting any real sympathy from the audience, and partly because the manner of his death, far from being lofty, borders on the farcical.

Lope knew perfectly well that the idea of Siquén and his men lying helpless after being circumcised had to get laughs

---

[93] The audience has watched all along the scheme of Jacob's sons to kill Siquén and all the men of the city.

from the boisterous spectators (*mosqueteros*), so he entered into the spirit of the thing by having Bato come rushing out onto the stage covered with flour from head to toe, proclaiming that he had been so frightened by the sight of the slain men that he had fallen headlong into a flour bin. There is no doubt that Lope was wise in anticipating the audience's reaction, for it would have been much worse if the spectators had laughed at a supposedly serious ending, but it is nevertheless a pity that he should have taken such pains to develop Siquén's character, only to dispose of him so unceremoniously at the end. Unfortunately Lope often chose to remain scrupulously faithful to his sources, even at the expense of his own creation.

Passion rewarded: Las justas de Tebas
("The Jousts of Thebes")

It would seem that the silent *sombra* was Lope's favorite device for causing passionate lovers to entertain forebodings about the future, for it appears in every one of the plays that are to be discussed in this chapter, with the sole exception of *La desdichada Estefanía.* The very fact that they are silent and give no specific information about the future (as did the dreams and prophecies) almost automatically causes the lovers to become introspective; they must ask themselves the questions that the *sombra* never formulates, and they must do what they can to penetrate the meaning of their supernatural experience. Introspection, of course, is an integral part of all passionate love, which depends a good deal on the intensity of the lover's imagination and on his ability to focus his mind on his own feelings and emotions. Capellanus emphasizes the role of imagination in the growth of amorous passion: "Not every kind of meditation can be the cause of love, an excessive one is required; for a restrained thought does not, as a rule, return to the mind, and so love cannot

arise from it."[94] The imagination of the lover, then, is excited
far beyond the normal bounds by his "excessive meditation,"
and so his visions or hallucinations are entirely appropriate.

It is also well known that fear is one of the dominant
features of passionate love, an emotion carefully stressed by
Capellanus and by the great majority of writers who have
dealt with the subject. The lover's fears are almost infinite:
he is afraid that his love might not be returned, that he might
be scorned, mocked, or spurned by his beloved, that a rival
might compete with him, that he might lose what he has tried
so hard to gain, that he might be separated forever from his
beloved, and so on. These fears are usually always present in
the mind of the lover, but fear itself is never so evident as in
the scenes in which *galán* and *sombra* confront each other,
for death then interposes itself as a new dimension of the
character's concerns.

We have seen that Siquén sensed that death was in store
for him by way of punishment for what he learned to accept
as his offense; he had sinned and the time for retribution was
near. His fear, of course, was fully justified, but the situation
itself had a moralistic ring and was consequently somewhat
unsubtle. The audience must have reacted to the foreshadowing of his looming death with a certain amount of compla-
cency, for a villain was being brought to account and justice
was being served.

In *Las justas de Tebas,* however, the protagonist Jelando
was in no way guilty of transgression. He loved a princess
and served her courteously; in return, she gave him as much
encouragement as her honor would allow. But the unfortunate suitor had a persistent rival, so the two men eventually
resolved to settle the matter in a duel. As the time for the
duel approached, Jelando was beset with forebodings. Siquén

[94] Andreas Capellanus, *The Art of Courtly Love,* ed. F.W. Locke, N.Y.
1957, pp. 2-3

saw a vision *de mi temor fabricada* ("created by my fear"), and now Jelando hears a mournful voice that seems to echo his own inner suffering. The question posed in the last two verses draws our attention to the core of the dramatic conflict: how can Jelando be saved from death if he so willingly risks his own life? He fears death with the intensity of one who has personal knowledge of it, and yet at the same time he is willing to sacrifice his life if it becomes necessary. Lope's characters have often stated that love does not fear death,[95] but this is not strictly true. What is really meant is that love is willing to risk death for the sake of the beloved, for not even life itself is of greater importance to the lover. Thus Jelando does nothing to avert the terrifying fate he foresees, and the spectators no doubt share his apprehension.

Soon the mournful voice outside his window is joined by the sound of heavy footsteps, and suddenly a *sombra* arrives. Jelando is in such a state of emotional excitement that he faints at the sight of the ghostly apparition. When he recovers, he tries to describe his experience to his servant:

> *¿Cómo puedo*
> *decirte lo que he visto a la ventana,*
> *si no es imagen de mi propio miedo?*
> *Sin duda que mi muerte ya es cercana.*
> (*Acad.* I, 263b)

("How can I tell you what I saw at the window if it's not the image of my own fear? Surely my death is drawing nigh.")

Jelando believes the specter is an objective embodiment of his own fear, and he correctly assumes that it portends death. But his servant chides him, warning him that if he cannot

---

[95] See Leonor's stance in "Amor no teme a la muerte," *La nueva victoria del marqués de Santa Cruz, Acad.* XIII, 56b, as one example in many.

control his emotions he will lose his honor and his life, as well as the respect his victories have brought him.

Once again we note the irony as the skeptical servant advises his master not to believe the omen of death, for both reader and audience know that he is fully justified in fearing the worst. Not only do bad omens come true on almost every occasion, but silent *sombras* are always seen to be heralds of death, for this belief was deeply rooted in the popular tradition of Lope's day.

There was one article of faith, however, that was always stronger than superstitious persuasions: the point of honor. In the section dealing with omens as devices of foreshadowing, it was pointed out that belief in omens was held to be contrary to the doctrines of the Church, and that such unorthodoxy was also considered a breech of honor. *"Esfuérzate, que pierdes honra y vida,"* Jelando's servant warns him grimly. ("Be strong and get control of yourself, or you will lose your honor and your life").[96] To lose one's honor is tantamount to losing one's life, for life without honor would be unbearable to Jelando or to any other nobleman worthy of the name. Life without the beloved, as has already been mentioned, would be equally unbearable, so love and honor merge as an ideal to which even life itself is subordinate. The true lover, like the true Christian, is a man of honor; everything else is secondary. Thus Jelando is forced, almost as if by the ancient *fatum*, to follow a course of action that will lead inevitably to his death.

The irony here is patently clear: if Jelando had been a lesser man he would have heeded the ghost's warning; but as a passionate lover and a man of honor he is doomed from the start. Lope the ironist was very canny in setting up this situation, for he knew his audience well enough to play off their superstitious beliefs against the theatrical tradition of love

---

[96] See previous page.

and honor. They believe in the ghosts and omens and thus they gain foreknowledge of the character's destiny, but the character himself cannot allow his actions to be influenced by warnings from beyond, and so he must courageously pursue his fatal path before the eyes of the fascinated spectators. His courage is all the greater because he, like the audience, also believes in the portents of doom (in all the plays we have studied so far, the agonist was initially scared by the omens before being persuaded to disregard them), so his conscious decision to put love and honor before fear and foreboding makes him a character of heroic, and sometimes tragic, proportions.

After listening closely to his servant's advice, Jelando swiftly recovers from his fear of the *sombra* when his honor is brought into question, and he resolves to kill his opponent during an upcoming joust. Jelando now begins to emerge not just as a courtly *galán* of a theatrical convention, but also as an incarnation of the knightly spirit found in the ever popular books of chivalry. One is particularly reminded of Don Quixote when Jelando accuses his rival of sending sorcerers to torment him; and, again like Don Quixote, his reaction is worthy of the finest tradition of knighthood, for he is all the more determined to conquer his rival in spite of *sombras* or sorcerers. The firmer his determination, however, the greater the audience's pity, for he is quixotically fighting against high odds, since his rival Ardenio is stronger, older, and more experienced than he.

The play might well have been a tragedy if Jelando had been its sole protagonist, and if his death had brought the action to a close. But Ardenio was also an important figure in the play, and after killing Jelando in the middle of the second act, he becomes the focus of the rest of the action. He is loved by Abderite, Queen of the Amazons, who, of course, has never deigned to love a man before. But like so many other characters in Lope's plays, her very invulnerability to passion suggests that she will soon become its victim. When she finally admits to her maidservant that she is in love with Ardenio, the girl is disgusted:

> *Cuanto ha que te conozco no me acuerdo*
> *verte con tal intento,*
> *que abominas siempre el casamiento.*
> *Perdona, Reina, si el respeto pierdo,*
> *que ese mortal cuidado*
> *es locura o veneno que te han dado.*

(Acad. I, 260b)

("In all the time I have known you, I do not recall your ever entertaining any such plan, for you have always despised the whole idea of marriage. Excuse me, Queen, if I lose all respect for you, but this inordinate concern of yours is either madness or some sort of poison they have given you.")

Abderite's passion for Ardenio is most unusual in Lope's theatre, for it seems to be almost totally disinterested. She realizes that Ardenio loves the Princess and plans to continue taking part in the joust (the winner will be given her hand in marriage), but Abderite never tries to dissuade him from fighting, even though his enthusiasm to win the joust is very painful to her. When he is wounded so badly that he can no longer continue, she disguises herself as a man and fights with greater skill and strength than all the other contestants put together, and in no time she wins the whole match. But when the moment comes for her to unmask herself, she steps gallantly aside and offers her prize to Ardenio. When the young man finds out what she has done for him, he is so moved by her unselfishness that he falls in love with her and decides to marry her. The Princess is thus liberated from any obligation, so she retires to her father's palace where she can remain faithful to the memory of Jelando.

The last act was written in a spirit of levity, and all turns out well in the end in true *Comedia* fashion. It is nevertheless an interesting example of how passion can be rewarded when it seeks not its own, and it is noteworthy that Abderite's love was perhaps closer to Pauline *caritas* than that of most of her counterparts on the Golden Age stage. From a dramatic point of view it is not surprising that *ēros* should predominate over *agapē,* for the conflicts and paradoxes inherent in the former made it an ideal subject for the theatre, not to mention the popular appeal it held for the audience. Yet few emotions, no matter how potentially untheatrical they might be, were out of Lope's range, for he always seemed to be able to create a dramatic situation where the partially hidden emotion could develop itself, while at the same time the action that surrounded it would hold the attention of the audience as well as maintain the tension of the play at a reasonably high level.

If Lope had written a dry sermon on Christian charity, his actors might have been pelted with tomatoes before his point could be made; instead, he entertained the audience with the incredible spectacle of a woman fighting for the sake of another woman so that she could marry the man she herself loved. Not until the end of the play did it become clear that her purpose was entirely altruistic. Lope's method of *enseñar deleitando*[97] was not only appropriate to the tastes and demands of his audience, but it was also particularly suitable to theatre as a genre, for on the stage character is best expressed through the action that encompasses it.

So while Lope sometimes allows the spectators to enjoy an ironic superiority over the characters in the more serious plays, he never really loses his control over what they may foresee and what will come as a surprise to them. He remains the supreme ironist, manipulating both audience and players with an artistry born of his deeply intuitive understanding of the *español sentado* (the seated Spaniard).

---

[97] "To teach while at the same time entertaining"—a Renaissance ideal that was enthusiastically embraced by Lope

Passion renounced: *La Santa Liga*
("The Holy League")

In Lope's theatre the renunciation of passion seems to be limited to characters of royal blood, as has already been noted in the previous discussions of *El príncipe perfecto* and *Las justas de Tebas.* This by no means implies that kings or potentates will always listen to reason and put honor and duty before passion (*Fuenteovejuna, Peribáñez, El príncipe despeñado,* and *El marqués de Mantua*), but generally we find that the order or harmony which is disturbed by them is eventually restored by other people.[98] This is the case in *La Santa Liga,* for Selín (*el Gran Turco*) is in love with Rosa Solimana, and spends most of his time with her instead of defending the lands that had cost his ancestors so many lives. After being warned by his advisers that his love is playing right into the hands of the Spaniards by making him neglectful of war, a silent and somehow respectful *sombra* appears before the astonished Selín:

---

[98] The theme of social harmony is dealt with at some length by Leo Spitzer, "A Central Theme and its Structural Equivalent in Lope's *Fuenteovejuna," HR,* XXIII, 1955, and by William C. McCrary, "*Fuenteofejuna:* Its Platonic Vision and Execution," *Studies in Philology,* LVIII, 1961. Both critics suggest that the main unity of action is to be found in its progress from "order disturbed" to "order restored", a movement which is particularly evident in Laurencia's growing love for and eventual spiritual union with Frondoso. This unity on a personal level is paralleled by the ultimate unification of *Fuente Ovejuna* itself under the banner of the Sovereigns, who in turn represent a newly unified Spain after the liberation of Ciudad Real. "The counterforce to Parker's observation that sedition and rape are dramatically unified in *Fuente Ovejuna* and represent 'aspects of an individual will to disorder' is the gradual realization of harmony expressed in terms of love and ultimate justice" (McCrary, p. 186). For Parker's comments on this question, see his "The Approach to the Spanish Drama of the Golden Age," *TDR,* IV, 1959.

Detente, aguarda: ¿adónde huyes, sombra?
Y si eres alma, aguarda un poco, espera;
Selín tu hijo soy, Selín te nombra;
Padre, ¿por qué te vas de esa manera?
Cuanto miro parece que me asombra;
Encógense los nervios y las cuerdas,
y pónese el cabello con las cerdas.

(*Acad.* XII, 325b)

("Stop, wait: why are you fleeing, shadow? And if you are a soul, tarry a while, wait; I am your son, Selín, Selín is calling you; Father, why are you leaving me this way? I am amazed by everything I see; my nerves and sinews are tight, and my hair is standing on end.")

Like the other passionate lovers now under discussion, Selín reacts fearfully to the presence of the ghost, but this time the hero has mixed feelings, for he perceives that the *sombra* is the spirit of his father, whose presence somehow clarifies Selín's understanding of his situation, causing him to become introspective. His conscience tells him his love for Solimana is a danger both to himself and to his kingdom. He feels that his concern for Solimana's whereabouts after a night of love is "an infamous notion," and unbecoming to his kingly sense of decorum. But unlike many of his passionate counterparts in Lope's theatre, Selín is able to renounce his love for the sake of his country.[99] Thus the order that was

---

[99] Halstead contends that lovers and persons of royal blood in Lope's plays are not able to resist the influence of the stars, which are often blamed for love's irresistible force (Frank G. Halstead, "The Attitude of Lope de Vega Toward Astrology," *HR,* VII, 1939, p. 208). But it is evident from the example above and from *Las paces de los reyes* that Lope would have us believe that man is sometimes capable of controlling his desire. As for his being able to control his destiny, man triumphs over the stars in *Contra valor no hay desdicha, Lo que ha de ser, Lo que está determinado, El hijo de los leones,* and *El servir con mala estrella.*

threatened by Selín's passionate love is once more restored, but Lope's interest in the Turk begins to dwindle toward the end of the second act, and Selín disappears entirely after the beginning of the third, which is devoted mainly to the praise of Don Juan de Austria and the victory at Lepanto, after the manner of the pageant play. Selín's position as a central figure in the play was doomed from the start, for as soon as he decided to follow the advice of the *sombra* and renounce his amorous passion, he also rid himself of any conflict that might have arisen from the clash between love and duty.

Passion renounced: *Las paces de los reyes*
("The Kings' Peace")

A similar situation occurs in *Las paces de los reyes,* for King Alfonso's love for Raquel is threatening the security of the nation very much in the same way that Selín's love for Rosa Solimana had jeopardized the safety of his people. When Selín was faced with the reproachful *sombra* of his father he quickly decided to give up his passion and concentrate his attention on matters of war, a decision that not only lacked psychological authenticity but also put a premature end to the inner conflict that gave dramatic tension to the play. King Alfonso, on the other hand, was not so easily persuaded to renounce his love for Raquel, so Lope bombarded him with warnings from beyond and foreshadowing of possible doom.

The first of these warnings came in the form of a well-known ballad that was sung to him by a mournful voice of unknown origin. The voice warns him that his behavior is displeasing to the king who made him (Alfonso) a king, and he further points out that he has even offended the celestial heavens. The voice goes on to remind him that heaven has protected him from his enemies ever since he was a boy, so he should endeavor to show his gratitude by reigning in his appetites now that he is a man.

Although the King seems to understand that his behavior
is displeasing to God and a danger to his country, he still
prefers to deceive himself into believing that the voice has
somehow been conjured up by his wife, Leonor, who is not
overly impressed by his dalliance with young Raquel. He
needs no skeptical confidante to talk him out of heeding the
warning voice—the blindness of his passion is sufficient. But
as soon as he convinces himself that the voice was nothing
but a trick, he is confronted by an actual *sombra con rostro
negro, túnica negra, espada y daga ceñida* (shadow with a
black face, a black tunic, and wearing both a dagger and a
sword). Like his many passionate counterparts, King Alfonso
is frightened by the *sombra,* which he thinks is the embodiment of his own fear, and which seems to be attempting to
prevent him from joining Raquel in a tryst.

The King's confidant is a rare character in Lope's plays,
for instead of displaying the usual skepticism about the protagonist's forebodings, he takes the side of the warning voice
and explains to Alfonso that the *sombra* appeared before him
because he was offending God. But the King persists in his
belief that it is all somehow part of his wife Leonor's witchcraft (echoes of Don Alonso), and he goes to see Raquel in
spite of everything. There is still a great deal of conflict in
his mind, however, because he admits that he has understood
the warnings when he says, *y perdida la razón,/ conozco el
daño, y le sigo* ("And having lost my reason/I am aware of
the harm, and yet I still pursue it." v.526). His self-awareness
makes him both an ironic figure and a potentially tragic one.

At the beginning of the third act there is an episode that
contains what might be called a piece of "traditional" foreshadowing—an episode which specifically foreshadows the
future action of the play. King Alfonso takes Raquel fishing,
and it occurs to them to offer each other whatever they might
happen to catch. She snags an olive branch for him, but
Alfonso finds to his horror that he has hooked a human skull.
Although this episode is rather melodramatic and the sym-

bolism somewhat too obvious, it is nevetheless ironic and yet deeply true to the nature of love that they should each be responsible for the other's fate. The two symbolic objects also serve to emphasize the underlying theme of the play: the restoration of peace and harmony and the triumph of justice for all through personal sacrifice and death.

The omen is soon fulfilled when Raquel is killed by some courtiers. The King gives way to a deeply felt outburst of grief when he hears the news, and he threatens to kill everybody who was involved in the crime, but he eventually does some soul-searching and finally repents, realizing that he must, from that point on, renounce his own desires for the sake of his kingdom. Queen Leonor forgives him and order is restored as the play comes to a close.

Lope's timing of the various stages of passionate love from its inception to the final *anagnōrisis* (sudden insight or awareness) was better in this play than in *La Santa Liga* ("The Holy League"), where, as we have seen, the third act was devoted to a description of a battle after the manner of the popular pageant plays. While it is true that in *Las paces de los reyes* the main action was delayed until the second act, this by no means makes the first act extraneous to the central theme, for Lope's portrayal of Alfonso's character as a boy sheds light on his behavior as a man. In the first act the young Alfonso is shown to be a courageous and judicious leader during the capture of Toledo, as well as a courteous and wise ruler after the city has been taken. His even-handed administration of justice makes him immensely popular with the people, but his decisions can sometimes be too rigorous: during the battle Dominguillo treacherously kills his master when he refuses to hand over his castle to Alfonso; later, when Dominguillo asks the King to reward him for his service, Alfonso grants him a yearly income from the treasury, but he also has the man's eyes put out as punishment for having turned against his master. This episode foreshadows things to come, for King Alfonso's austere sense of justice will eventually be directed toward himself when he learns to accept the death of Raquel and assume reponsibility for the well-being of his kingdom.

Passion as jealousy: *La desdichada Estefanía* ("The Sorrowful Stephanie")

Although the main action of this play does not unfold until the middle of Act Two, the introductory scenes nonetheless prepare the audience for the tragic ending by carefully establishing the character of the central figures, Fortunio and Castro. The two men are enemies from the very start: Castro, who serves King Alfonso VII of Castille, angrily accuses Fortunio (a nobleman in the court of the King of France) of aggravating a misunderstanding between the two monarchs, and he challenges him to a duel. Estefanía, King Alfonso's daughter and Castro's secret fiancée, is worried about the duel and begs her lover to be on his guard.

When Fortunio fails to appear at the appointed time and place, Castro returns to Castile only to find that his rival is just about to marry Estefanía, a union arranged by the two kings as a means of sealing their newly-sworn friendship. Castro is outraged and demands justice from King Alfonso, telling him that he is already betrothed to Estefanía. The King is moved by his impassioned plea and marries the lovers then and there, leaving Fortunio in a state of despair, not only because he truly loves Estefanía himself, but also because Castro had accused him of cowardice for not showing up at the duel, an accusation which could never be erased even though he presented a good excuse for his unavoidable absence.

This is how matters stand in the middle of the second act. Castro—arrogant, violent and impulsive—has succeeded in bringing order to his own affairs and is satisfied about the state of his honor. Fortunio—passionate, affronted, angry and frustrated—is at his wit's end and still yearns to possess

Estefanía despite the wedding and her constant rebuffs. At this point Lope takes up the tale as it is recounted by Fr. Prudencio de Sandoval in *La Crónica del Emperador Don Alonso VII.*[100] Isabel, Estefanía's maidservant, is in love with Fortunio (a fact well established from the beginning), and it occurs to her to disguise herself as her mistress in order to deceive Fortunio into making love to her in the dark of night. She tells Fortunio that Estefanía loves him and wants to meet him in the garden. He is so delighted by this unexpected news that he agrees to the arrangements without hesitation.

Now that the audience has been prepared for an unhappy outcome, Lope uses various devices of foreshadowing to fortify the sense of doom and to give the characters an awareness of the dark events lying ahead. Thus the characters feel disturbed when Estefanía falls as she leaves the church, and they find it no less unsettling to learn that Castro's house has spontaneously caved in, killing four of his servants:

Castro:	*Algo me ha de suceder.*
Estefanía:	*Algún daño se me acerca.*

* * *

Ramiro:	*No temas que suceda lo que dices;*
	que estas son cosas naturales todas.
Alfonso:	*Ramiro, ¡plega a Dios! Pero en efeto*
	si contra nuestra fe no fuera
	creer en agüeros, diera a todo crédito;
	mas estas cosas son muy naturales.

(Acad. VIII, 351b)

---

[100] Menéndez y Pelayo also suggests as a possible source the *Tragedias de amor,* written in 1604 by Juan de Arce Solórzano, but Sandoval's account (written in 1600) seems to provide most of the details. For a full reproduction of the Sandoval version, see Pelayo's introduction in *Acad.* VIII.

| Castro: | Something is bound to happen to me. |
| Estefanía: | Something bad is coming my way. |

* * *

Ramiro:	Don't worry about things like that;
	For these are all natural occurrences.
Alfonso:	Ramiro, pray God that it be so! But in fact
	if it were not against our religion
	to believe in omens, I would believe it all;
	but these are very natural occurrences.

(*Acad.* VIII, 351b)

The audience, from its privileged distance, sees the irony inherent in the conflict between the characters' faith in Catholic dogma and their well-founded misgivings about the future. The characters suspect that something is amiss, but the spectators, knowing more than they, observe them with fear and trembling as they dig their own graves.

The action reaches a climax in the third act, which opens with the meeting of Fortunio and Isabel in the garden. The spectators have watched one of Castro's servants spying on them throughout their rendezvous, so Fortunio's enraptured words to his servant must fill them with foreboding as he plans for a future wedding. Fortunio is aware of the danger, but for that very reason he is more than ever committed to following the dictates of his desire. "*Y perdida la razón, conozco el daño, y le sigo.*" ("And having lost my reason, I know the danger, and I follow it.") His foreknowledge makes his decision all the more tragic as he consciously forfeits life for passionate love.

Castro, warned by his servants that his honor is in jeopardy, hides himself in the garden to await the arrival of the lovers. His willingness to believe in his wife's unproven guilt is not surprising to the audience, for we have seen that Lope carefully delineated the essential characteristics of his personality from the beginning. Castro's arrogance not only suggests a tragic *hubris*, but it also provides the necessary psychological preparation for his jealousy and eventual violence. His feud with his enemy also adds to the inevitability of the ending, for he can never be sure that the man who came so close to marrying his wife does not still harbour some love for her.[101] With these factors in mind, the audience watches Castro's mounting fury with special apprehension, fully aware that this Othello-like figure is involving himself and those around him in a tragic drama.

As soon as Castro sees Isabel (whom he takes to be his wife) and Fortunio together in the garden, he rushes at his rival and kills him in one stroke, but not before Isabel has had an opportunity to run back into the house, where she takes refuge under the bed of her mistress. Castro dashes into the bedroom and mortally wounds Estefanía before she has a chance to say a single word in her own defense. As she dies, however, she forgives Castro for his crime, and sorrowfully reproaches him for his mad and unjust violence.

After committing the fatal deed, Castro grows conscious of his temporary madness, and he blames the power of his passionate violence on the influence of the stars, or perhaps on some inner demons whose promptings he cannot fully understand. Suddenly Isabel makes a noise under the bed, and when Castro finally understands his terrible mistake, he expresses his sorrow with words of whole-hearted grief.

Although the foreshadowing was less pronounced in this play than in the ones where silent *sombras* evoked in the terrified lovers a mixture of foreboding and self-awareness, it is Castro's final *anagnōrisis*, rather than a growing self-

---

[101] In Sandoval's version the maidservant is not visiting Castro's rival in the garden, but rather a lover of her own who has no connection with the master of the house. It is by happenstance, and not by plan, that she is dressed in the clothes of her mistress. Thus Castro's jealousy has much more foundation and is far more understandable (and hence more tragic) in Lope's play than in Sandoval's rendition.

consciousness and inner conflict, that makes him a tragic character. He is devastated by the recognition of what he has done, and even though the King does not sentence him to death, the audience knows that he will always have to live with the burden of his knowledge and his terrible loss. Vossler has correctly described this play as being "la obra que se acerca más a la pura tragedia," (the play that comes the closest to being a pure tragedy),[102] for the ending leaves us to contemplate the painful spectacle of human suffering without offering us the optimistic note of relief which is generally to be found in the final verses of even the most somber of Lope's plays.

The conflict of passion and reason:
La imperial de Otón
("The Empire of King Otto")

This admirable play is among Lope's earliest dramatic efforts, written probably toward the end of 1597.[103] It is not without structural flaws (the tempo is interrupted in the first act by the introduction of a blustery Spanish grandee whose main purpose is to provide the audience with at least *one* national figure to cheer for in this *comedia de asunto extranjero* (play set in a foreign land), but poetic diction, character development, and dramatic conflict are all handled with remarkable skill. Not the least of its merits is the attention that Lope pays to the technique of foreshadowing and the consequent development of irony and tragic dilemma. His skillful

---

[102] Karl Vossler, *Lope de Vega y su tiempo* (trad. Ramón de la Serna), Madrid, 1933, p. 313.

[103] Morley and Bruerton suggest 1598, but Diego Marín (*La intriga secundaria en el teatro de Lope de Vega,* Mexico, 1958) upholds the earlier date.

manipulation of these devices is noteworthy in such an early play, for it bears witness to the fact that he was intuitively aware of their dramatic potential right from the start, and continued to be so throughout his career.[104]

Lope found the material for this play in an account by Pedro Mexía,[105] in which the popular historian describes how, after years of quarreling and political maneuvering, Count Rudolph of Hapsburg was finally elected Emperor of Germany. His election infuriated King Ottokar of Bohemia, because Rudolph had once been his vassal, so the idea of doing obeisance to his former subordinate was repugnant to him and violated his sense of honor. He accordingly sent messengers to the new Emperor telling him that he did not recognize the legality of the elections and would therefore not turn over his lands to him. Rudolph immediately mobilized his forces and marched on Austria, where he was met by King Ottokar's troops. But during the time that the two armies were standing face-to-face waiting for a signal from their leaders, certain monks and other holy men quickly interceded, and by dint of many persuasive conferences they managed to reconcile the hostile parties. It was finally agreed that Rudolph would forgive the King for his insubordination if he handed over all his lands, with the exception of Bohemia and Moravia, and if he also came personally to his camp to swear obedience in the customary way. Otto accepted these terms on condition that the ceremony be private and carried out in a secret place, so that nobody might see him humble himself before his former vassal. A special tent was erected for the purpose, but just as King Ottokar was doing

---

[104] See the Appendix, where those plays containing specific foreshadowing are arranged in chronological order.

[105] *Historia Imperial y Cesárea... Madrid, 1655,* pp. 515-519. See Menéndez y Pelayo, *Estudios sobre el teatro de Lope de Vega,* pp. 281-286, where the account is reproduced in full.

homage to Rudolph on bended knee, the flaps of the tent were suddenly drawn open in such a way that he became visible to all the soldiers in the field. Although Ottokar was deeply humiliated by this piece of treachery, he nevertheless returned to his palace with his army.

There he was greeted by his enraged Queen, who accused him of cowardice, weakness, and (worst of all) dishonorable conduct. She even went so far as to demand that he turn over his army to her, so that she might march at the head of the batallion and challenge Rudolph herself. King Otto was so agitated by her words that he decided to fight Rudolph after all, but during the battle he was killed on the field by one of the Emperor's servants, and so he died an ignominious death.

These are the facts as an historian has told them, but many details not relevant to the play have been omitted here. Lope, however, takes these historical facts and turns them into dramatic poetry by concentrating on the form and meaning of the chain of events. He emphasizes the character of the King and Queen, revealing their motivations through an examination of the way they react to their circumstances and to each other. He dwells on the power of love and ambition, he unmasks the protagonist's inner conflicts through the various devices of foreshadowing, and he discloses the ironic nature of Otón's fate with his careful manipulation of the audience's foreknowledge of the events which lead to his inevitable doom.

Despite Lope's introduction of one or two irrelevant historical facts, his general handling of the main lines of the action serves as a good illustration of Aristotle's comment that poetry can be "a more philosophical and higher thing than history: for poetry tends to express the universal, history the particular." Thus Lope stresses the irony of Otón's tragic destiny from the first moment he appears on the stage. He enters with his servants in a state of great agitation, for he has just learned that one of his favorite falcons was killed during the hunt by another bird of prey. The spectators are put on the alert by the very clear symbolism of this portent, for the wild bird of prey was *un ave vil,* a bird of "lesser rank" as it were, so they are warned by this omen of what lies in store for Otón, since they already know that Count Rodolfo has been elected Emperor. But the King and the Queen have not yet been informed of the outcome of the elections, so their reactions to the strange hunting accident are full of ironical overtones that are, of course, understood only by the audience. Queen Etelfrida, however, is partially aware of the meaning of the ominous accident, and she expresses her clairvoyant doubts to her husband:

> Etelfrida: *Haber visto*
> *matar una ave ratera*
> *un halcón de tal manera,*
> *que el llanto apenas resisto.*
> *Y hame dado mal agüero*
> *de que no os han elegido*
> *y en vuestro lugar lo ha sido*
> *algún príncipe extranjero.*
>
> (*Aguilar* III, 576a)

("After seeing [hearing about] a vile scavenger bird killing a noble falcon that way, I can hardly keep from weeping. I think it is a bad omen which warns me that you were not elected after all. Instead of you [in your place] they have elected some foreign prince.")

Lope's Otón responds in a predictable manner if we keep in mind what has already been said about omens and the reactions they elicit: one character is always troubled by the inauspicious implications of the omen, while the other one always reacts with skepticism or disbelief. This dramatic stratagem serves the same purpose every time: the doubts of the troubled character forewarn the audience and often raise

conflicts in the character himself, but the skeptical character's carefree attitude serves to deceive both himself and the
other characters into acting with the sort of false confidence
that ironically leads them right into the trap.

Otón's reaction, then, is one of disbelief, but a disbelief
which is touching because it reveals a disarming trust in
human nature:

> Otón: *No os dé pena, ¡por mi vida!*
> *Segura está mi elección*
> *donde interés o pasión*
> *no puede ser admitida.*
> *Son los electores nobles*
> *y conocen mi poder.*
>
> (*Aguilar* III, 576a)

("Don't let it trouble you, for heaven's sake! My election is
safeguarded by men who do not allow themselves to be influenced by emotion or self-interest. The electorate is made
up of noblemen, and they know my power.")

But the spectators have already witnessed the self-interested
squabbling of the supposedly noble electorate, so the irony
of King Otón's trusting words are not lost on them. As for
Queen Etelfrida, she has little patience for his idealism:

> Etelfrida: *En los nobles suele haber*
> *muchas veces tratos dobles.*
> *No lo habéis solicitado*
> *como el caso requería;*
> *si el que pide no porfía,*
> *duerme el que da, descuidado.*
>
> (*Aguilar* III, 576a)

("Noblemen often tend to be two-faced. You did not ask for
their help in the proper way; if the solicitor is not persistent,
the [potential] donor simply shrugs and falls asleep.")

Otón insists on believing that the best man must surely win, a false notion that leads him to interpret the omen in a way which is favorable to his case: the falcon, he maintains, represents the kings of England and Spain, two proud and capable men who have been competing for the Empire; but the so-called scavenger bird represents himself, for he has been humble and retiring in his struggle for the Empire (with the expectation that he would be elected for his own intrinsic value), so the victory of the *ave ratera* (literally "rat-catcher bird") over the falcon is a good omen, indicating his own imminent election. The irony of Otón's misinterpretation of the omen is clearly evident to the audience; perhaps somewhat less evident is the fact that his apparent humility is really an inverted *hubris,* so certain is he that the Empire will soon rest in his worthy hands.

Shortly after this episode a messenger presents himself before King Otón and the Queen and announces that Count Rodulfo has been elected Emperor. King Otón is practically speechless, but the Queen is by no means at a loss for words. After the inevitable "I told you so," *No era, señor, mi recelo tan vanamente creído,* 576b ("Never, sir, were my suspicions given so little credence"), she goes on to demand that her husband take up arms against Rodulfo, threatening to lead the army herself if he refuses, and further threatening him with the withdrawal of all favors, love, and respect if he feels disinclined to carry out her wishes.

King Otón immediately complies with this extraordinary ultimatum, rallying his troops and inciting them to march against the new Emperor for the sake of Bohemia's honor. The humility of which he boasted earlier seems to melt away in the excitement of his speech:

> *La corona imperial tendrá mi frente,*
> *y el sacro Imperio mis valientes hombros,*
> *que tengo hombros y hombres para todo.*
> (*Aguilar* III, 577b)

("I shall wear the imperial crown proudly on my head, and I shall bear the sacred Empire on my shoulders, for I have men and shoulders enough to get the job done.")

Queen Etelfrida knows exactly how to manipulate him by promising to love him only if he carries out her ambitious and unjust demands, claiming all the while that what moves her is his display of "courage" and "honorable anger." Lope, aware no doubt that his portrayal of Otón's overly-obliging character might be poorly received by his spectators (who had their own, rather commonplace ideas of what a king should be), quickly began to emphasize Otón's role as lover over his role as King, so his willing compliance to his wife's demands would not be mistaken for weakness unbefitting a royal personage. As a lover, Otón was naturally concerned about Etelfrida's opinion of him, and he was willing to do anything at all to gain her respect and admiration, so he served her and dutifully carried out her wishes just as any courtly lover would have done for his lady. Lope's emphasis of Otón's passionate love for Etelfrida accomplishes another purpose as well, for it helps explain the King's initial blindness to the morally questionable goal of his military enterprise.[106] Having been asked by his ambitious and unscrupulous wife to attack the new Emperor, the devoted King Otón marched off to battle without a thought as to whether or not he was undertaking a just cause. As a lover, he is blind to the injustice of his military aggression, but as King, he will be unable to disregard either its implications or its possible consequences. This conflict soon becomes the core of the dramatic tension, and ultimately leads to his tragic death.

---

[106] Although the electors were a quarrelsome and self-serving group of men, there is nothing in either Mexía's or Lope's accounts to indicate that the elections were in any way illegal.

When the two armies are finally lined up for battle, Merlin appears on the stage dressed as an old hermit, and he announces to Rodulfo that he has nothing to fear from his enemies. He will not only win the battle, but he will some day bring glory to Spain through his progeny, many of whom will belong to the House of Hapsburg. Merlin's prophecy clearly invites the audience to place its sympathy with Rodulfo, who now becomes the prototype of the fearless warrior-king who appealed so much to the average spectator. Once again Lope has found a way to liberate himself from the necessity of presenting Otón as a stock character for the purpose of pleasing his audience and fulfilling its expectations. Now that Rodulfo can play the part of "national hero," Lope is free to develop those aspects of Otón's behavior that would otherwise be unacceptable in a strong and admired King: confusion, fear, indecision and a surfeit of complaisance. Thus Otón emerges as one of the most interesting and original characters in Lope's repertoire, as well as one of the most sympathetic—for it is love that inspires an eagerness to please, a strong conscience that makes him indecisive, a sense of justice that causes him to fear the implications of his actions, and a courageous self-awareness that makes him prey to the forebodings that are to worry him all his life.

The plethora of conflicting emotions merges in a crisis of dramatic tension immediately after Merlin foreshadows the ending with his prediction, for just as Otón is readying himself for battle, there appears before him a *sombra* with his sword sheathed. The very fact that the *sombra*'s sword remains in its scabbard shows that he is not threatening Otón but he *is* asking him to do a little serious soul-searching. The passage (585b-586b) sheds light on the function and meaning of the silent *sombras* who so frequently appear before the terrified protagonists. We have seen that in each case the characters who see the specters are usually already troubled by an uneasy conscience, so their initial fear is not so much a reaction to the supernatural as it is a manifestation of their own inner conflict when faced with an accuser.[107] On the one hand they brazenly challenge the *sombra* in an attempt to protest their innocence, and on the other hand the presence of the ghost causes them to face with greater honesty the conflict they were hoping to deny or overlook. Thus Otón, after calling his servants to help him banish the specter, ends up acquiring real insight into the meaning of his fear and oppression. He now clearly understands that he has no right to challenge his just opponent, and he correctly interprets the *sombra* as being a heavenly warning to this effect.

During the entire passage Toledo (the pompous nobleman mentioned at the beginning of this section) makes a series of comments that not only reveal his superficial understanding of Otón's dilemma, but also reflect the sort of mindless patriotic attitude that must have been well received by the audience. He encourages Otón to attack Rodulfo for the illogical reason that he has a strong army and "un Toledo de España" to help him in this enterprise. But Otón cannot subscribe to the theory that "might makes right," so he turns away from the commonplae morality of the crowd and decides to negotiate peace with his so-called enemy.

Toledo's reaction to the King's spiritual victory is quite predictable: he believes it to be a poorly disguised demonstration of cowardice, and he turns his back on this monarch whom he now considers to be unworthy of his respect. It is hardly necessary to stress the irony of Toledo's opinion, for it is clear that what the Spaniard interprets as cowardice is in reality a demonstration of moral courage, for incited by the

---

[107] At no time were the protagonists frightened by the *vocal* variety of ghost. Only the silent specters, pointing a symbolic finger at their victims, elicited from them feelings of fear and sometimes remorse. There are certain coincidental parallels between this play and *Macbeth* (the characters of Etelfrida and Lady Macbeth, for example), not the least of which is the silent and accusing figure of Banquo's ghost and the *sombra* that appears in this play.

apparition of the silent *sombra,* Otón has finally come to see himself and his motives as they really are.

This moment of insight is dramatically emphasized in a curious conversation between Otón and his confidant Alberto at the beginning of Act Three. They are trying to discover some "scientific" explanation for the appearance of the silent *sombra,* and Alberto comes up with a certain Aristotelian (according to him) theory which describes how men, when they are very weak or frightened, sometimes see a mirror image of themselves before their eyes.[108]

Otón's extreme emotional stress before the battle might account for his having seen his double, but in Lope's plays it would seem that the mirror image reflects much more than the physical self or an emotional state. It seems, indeed, to reflect what could be called the viewer's "true" self, or perhaps his higher nature. In every case that we have studied so far, the protagonist emerges from this experience with a self-awareness that was lacking before the *sombra* appeared. Siquén became conscious for the first time of his *agravio,* Jelando realized that his love was doomed, King Alfonso admitted "*y perdido la razón, conozco el daño, y le sigo.*" Otón's case is original in that he has the courage to act on his new insight by refusing to fight, whereas the other lovers mentioned above were unable to come to terms with their knowledge, a fact which directly or indirectly brought about tragic results. What is even more tragic about Otón, how-

---

[108] Irving Babbitt (*Rousseau and Romanticism,* 1919; republished by Meridian Books, Ohio, 1966) mentions the fascination that the phenomenon of the double (Doppelganger) had for Hoffmann and other German Romantics (p. 204). He refers the reader to Brandes, *The Romantic School in Germany,* ch. XI, and also makes the following observations: "Alfred de Musset saw his double in the stress of his affair with George Sand (see *Nuit de Décembre*), Jean Valjean sees his double in the stress of his conversion. Peter Bell also sees his double at the emotional crisis in Wordsworth's poem of that name" (n. 18, p. 313).

ever, is that he ultimately turns his back on what he had once accepted as a just and righteous decision, and he pays the consequences with the full knowledge of what he has done. In light of what has been said about the function of silent *sombras* then, it would be difficult to accept Pelayo's hasty assertion that "esta sombra es el *deus ex machina* que determina la súbita cobardía de Otón, el cual sin combatir se entrega a Rodulfo."[109] Further proof of the fact that his motivating force is not cowardice but rather a sincere moral conviction can be found in his reaction to Rodulfo's betrayal. When the flaps of the tent are suddenly drawn open to reveal King Otón in a humiliating position at the feet of his former vassal, he is still able to swallow the insult without abandoning his decision not to fight.

Otón has been undeniably affronted by Rodulfo's symbolic slap in the face, yet despite his loss of honor, he cannot bring himself to take up arms against his enemy. In continuing to act according to his conscience, he must of necessity go against the honor code that dictated the behavior of his

---

[109] *Estudios sobre el teatro de Lope de Vega*, p. 292. Menéndez Pelayo seems to agree with Farinelli's general position on the subject of Otón's so-called cowardice (see *Grillparzer und Lope de Vega*, Berlin, 1894, pp. 65-78), but Vossler, in the two paragraphs that he dedicates to this play, shows that he has understood the role that passion plays in Otón's behavior (*Lope de Vega y su tiempo*, p. 316): "A mi modo de ver, Lope ha querido dar un sentido distinto a su rey de Bohemia, proponiéndose personificar en él a una criatura dotada de grandeza, nobleza, y valor, a quien las ambiciones de su esposa, con exceso amada, empujan a la sinrazón. No acceder a las súplicas de una mujer como Etelfrida, fuera cobardía: *Porque, en fin, es de cobardes/Ser con las mujeres valientes.* Este axioma caballeresco, que tantas veces ha exaltado Lope, presta a su rey Otón el ímpetu, incluso la petulancia que necesita para aventurarse en el terreno de lo ilegal o imposible…Los remordimientos que restaron firmeza al brazo del héroe—de ninguna manera pusilánime, sino desapoderado y temerario—los ha materializado Lope en forma de reflexiones y dudas que surgen en su intimidad."

dramatic counterparts in the Golden Age theatre, and in so doing he inevitably invites the spectators to take a scornful view of what they must consider to be his abject cowardice. This ready-made explanation of Otón's behavior has already been voiced by the arrogant Don Juan de Toledo, and it will be repeated by the warlike Etelfrida, but these characters are limited creatures, products of a literary and theatrical convention whose rules they never hesitate to follow. Otón, however, is a highly original character who challenges convention by refusing to obey the rules, but unlike other defiant characters in Lope's theatre, his challenge probably fails to capture the sympathy of the audience. Commoners who stood up to their oppressors in defiance of rigid social conventions were enthusiastically supported by their theatre viewers; countless lovers whose passion led them to violate the marital conventions were appreciated and forgiven by the spectators (even though the play itself demanded that justice be served), but a leader who chose not to engage the enemy, no matter what his reasons, was bound to be misunderstood in Lope's day, when military fervor was greatly admired.

Thus Otón is constantly excoriated by the characters who represent traditional heroism: Toledo deserts him after declaring that such a "pusilánime príncipe y cobarde/no hará cosa jamás que buena sea" (586b), and Rodulfo accuses him of "infamia y cobardía" (590a). But the most scathing vituperation of all comes from Queen Etelfrida, who mounts one of the turrets of the castle and appears before him dressed in full armor. She refuses to allow him and his men to enter the castle, claiming that their presence within its walls would rob her of her honor. She calls him an "hombre vil," fit only for sewing and other household chores. He is, she continues, infamous, cowardly, dishonorable, weak, and effeminate... finally she threatens to lead his army herself if he cannot, or will not, attack Rodulfo. Her words have their intended effect on Otón:

Cesen ya las palabras afrentosas,
valerosa Etelfrida, que te juro
por el supremo autor que rige el cielo,
por mi real corona y por tus ojos,
que son las piedras y diamantes de ella,
de no entrar en mi casa, ni quitarme
la espada en Praga, ni comer bocado,
hasta volver en busca de Rodulfo;
venci óme tu valor, que nuevamente
dentro del pecho corazón me infunde;
conocí mi flaqueza y cobardía,
y pagaréla con verter mi sangre.

(*Aguilar* III, 594a)

("No more insulting words, valiant Etelfrida, for I swear to you by the supreme Author who rules Heaven above, and by my royal crown and by your eyes—which are the most precious stones and diamonds [in the crown]—by these I swear to you that I will not enter my house, nor put aside my sword in Prague, nor eat one mouthful of food until I set out to seek Rodulfo again. I have been won over by your bravery, which once again fills my breast with determination. I realize I am weak and cowardly, and I'll spill my blood to pay for that.")

This time King Otón's change of mind is an act of love, and if he appears to have quickly forgotten the moral insight the silent *sombra* inspired in him, it is simply because lovers tend to see themselves through the eyes of the beloved. Otón had been called a coward and a weakling before, but now that Etelfrida has repeated the accusation, he accepts her judgment without question, anxious only to prove to her that he can overcome his so-called cowardice and live up to the image of what she wants him to be, even though he foresees that it will cost him his life. One cannot help but see in this desperate about-face another example of King Alfonso's "y perdida la razón/ conozco el daño y le sigo," ("And having

lost my reason/I am aware of the wrong, and I pursue it.")—
an insight which could easily serve as a *Leitmotiv* for almost
every one of Lope's tragic figures, endowed as they are with
a foreknowledge that cannot prevent them from becoming
victims of their own inevitable fates.

The concepts of courage and cowardice are not easy to
define, nor is it always possible to keep the two qualities
from merging with each other within the same character. A
man can be courageous and decisive when inspired by hope
or insight, and yet totally lack even the slightest vestige of
courage on another occasion when he feels deeply confused
or threatened. So it is with Otón, whose initial courage gave
him the strength not to attack Rodulfo even after being
insulted in front of both armies, and despite full knowledge
of the honor code. But his second sally, like his first, is
prompted not so much by a sudden mustering of courage as
it is by a passionate need to be loved and respected by the
Queen. The very fact that his decision to attack is so hasty
and compulsive makes his underlying fear and frustration
almost self-evident. He must go against his better judgment
for the sake of the woman he loves, and the only way to do
this is to take a sudden plunge, a decision which is ironically
applauded by even his closest confidant. Ataúlfo assures him
that *ese valor es digno de tu pecho* ("Now your courage is
worthy of you" 594a), and the Queen praises him once more:
*Ahora quiero yo darte mis brazos,/ ahora eres, Otón, mi bien
y mi esposo* ("Now I want to take you in my arms, now you
are, Otón, my love and my husband" 594a).

Unfortunately the mere decision to act is easily mistaken
for courage, while a refusal to do so is often seen as cowardice. In Otón's case, however, the opposite is true, which con-
stitutes the central irony of the entire play. What moves us to
the classical pity and terror is our knowledge that King Otón
himself shares our insight. The recognition of the forewarned
protagonist is perhaps better expressed in this play than in
any other in Lope's repertoire. Otón is thoroughly aware of

the inadvisability of this second attack. He recognizes the uselessness of bloodshed, he mourns the loss of his men whom he has led to the battle like lambs to the slaughter, and he is aware of the power of passionate love, against which reason has only rarely been known to prevail. Above all, he understands that his dilemma is part of the human condition, as his wide perspective and historical sense make clear. He is a philosopher miscast in the role of a general, a poet who is forced against his will to undertake a campaign which is repugnant to him. Finally he is a lover resigned to his fate, and willing to sacrifice everything for his beloved.

Then, just as he is about to enter the fray, the *sombra* reappears and seizes him by the arm, but Otón shakes him off, unwilling to listen to his urgent warnings. He is not only physically exhausted by his trips back and forth from castle to battleground, but emotionally exhausted from weighing moral subtleties in his mind, a task which entailed as many different decisions as trips. While in a state of exhaustion men and women can be driven to undertake wreckless or heroic deeds, resigned as they are by sheer fatigue to accept the consequences, and it is in this frame of mind that Otón, spurred on by his passionate love for Etelfrida, goes to his death. Neither the *sombra,* nor reason, nor the demands of his conscience hold sway now over his tragic resignation. He is mortally wounded by a lowly soldier who does not even realize he is the King, and so the prophecy in the episode of the falcon and the scavenger bird (the *ave vil*, see p. 131) is fulfilled. Lope treats his death with sympathy, inserting in his last soliloquy certain well-known refrains from the ballad about the Marqués de Mantua:

> *¿Dónde estás, señora mía,*
> *causa de todo mi mal?*
>
> (*Aguilar* III, 595b)

("Where are you, my lady, the cause of all my trouble?")

Etelfrida arrives just as Otón is commending his soul to God, too late for him to recognize her or receive any comfort from her presence, but his thoughts were with her to the end. He has sacrificed his life for her sake and for her honor, a gift which does not go unappreciated by the demanding, forceful Queen. The rigorous rules of the honor code required that he die, but perhaps the most ironic aspect of his death lies in the fact that he was only then able to win his wife's love:

Etelfrida: *Aunque el mundo me disfame*
de ver que muerto te ame,
como ya, mi bien, lo estás,
digo que te quiero más
mil veces muerto que infame.

(*Aguilar* III, 596b)

("Even if people speak ill of me when they see I love you now that you are dead, I still say that I love you a thousand times more dead than infamous.")

King Otón's marriage was obviously not a marriage in the conventional sense, but rather a long and often tormented courtship in which the hopeful yet despairing lover woos his *belle dame san merci,* for whom he undertakes even the most impossible deeds. Queen Etelfrida must be one of the most demanding and least merciful ladies in Lope's entire theatre, awesome qualities for which she is rewarded by the dedicated service of her loyal and admiring husband. The devices of foreshadowing warn him constantly of the risks involved in fullfilling his lady's demands, yet despite full knowledge of these dangers (and to some extent *because* of them) he is driven by his passion to make the supreme sacrifice. This he does willingly, but he cannot forget that he is not only a lover but also a King, and he sorrowfully laments the loss of his soldiers who died for the sake of a woman (*y todo por*

una mujer). Although he has proven to be a noble and even a
heroic lover, he has still failed as a king, for he has sacrificed
the lives of his men to a cause which he had always recognized as unjust. The honor code ironically exonerates him,
but his experience with the silent *sombra* has led him to see
far more clearly than before, so he becomes the tragic victim
of a fate he foresaw but could not, and would not, attempt to
modify.

The tragedy of passion:
El caballero de Olmedo
("The Knight of Olmedo")

It is appropriate to end this chapter with an examination of *El
caballero de Olmedo,* a play that is without a doubt one of
Lope's most spectacular achievements, for it unites and dramatizes not only the various topics that have been covered so
far, but it also makes use of certain themes and devices that
lend themselves to a further development of the main lines of
this thesis. In any case, no other play is better suited to an in-
vestigation of the way in which irony and foreshadowing are
used to dramatize the tragic and paradoxical nature of erotic
love, for Don Alonso, like many other lovers in the pages of
Spanish literature, devoted all his energies and force of imagination to the service of his lady, only to find that his most
cherished fantasies were doomed by prosaic reality.

   This chapter has attempted to point out the various conflicts that arose within the characters as a result of their amorous passion: we have seen how Jelando struggled with his
awareness of imminent death, how Siquén was tormented by
the realization that his passion had driven him to mistreat his
beloved, how King Alfonso was torn between love and duty,
how Castro had to live with the knowledge of his unbearable
mistake, and finally, how Otón fought to bring into harmony
the demands of reason and desire.

El caballero de Olmedo, however, will be of special interest because it offers a particularly vivid example of how passion itself carries within it a series of paradoxes that are independent of outside factors, and which in themselves suffice to bring about dramatic conflict. It is no longer entirely a question of love and duty, or reason and desire; it now becomes a question of how to keep passion alive when, in spite of the lovers' yearning for intimacy and union, it perversely demands obstacles, separation, absence, and finally, death. The paradoxes of passion force the lovers to play a game whose rules they accept with a sort of melancholy resignation as they follow the road to their doom; but it is their own awareness of their commitment to an ultimately destructive force that makes their deaths tragic. They cannot abandon the game, so they must become its victims.

The story of passionate love and its mysterious culmination in death has been a popular theme in European literature since the end of the eleventh century. At that time an entirely new philosophy of love found its way into the songs of the troubadours, a love based on the now familiar tenets of *l'amour courtois.*[110] With Chrétien de Troyes there was added to the old chivalric code the new ideal of *Frauendienst,* a serious type of heresy because it put the adoration of women before that of God.

According to this ideal, the lover is first a *fenhedor* (timid lover), worshipping his lady but never daring to let her know the love he feels. His *amour lointain* (love from afar) causes him to feel blessed suffering, and he spends his time thinking of her longingly. Soon he is driven by his passion to the next stage, that of *precador* (supplicant), at which point he begs his lady to let him love her. In accordance with the

---

[110] This term was first applied by Gaston Paris. See F.W. Locke's introduction to Andreas Capellanus, *The Art of Courtly Love,* N.Y., 1957, p.vi

rules of the game, the lady gives no sign of interest, for she is a *belle dame sans merci* (a beautiful, merciless lady). The man then becomes an *amant désespéré* (desperate lover) because of the lofty disinterest of his lady, and he often develops the lovers' disease of *hereos*. Yet all the time he is savoring the blessed suffering of having been rejected, and he secretly admires the *superiorité de la dame* who has not deigned to cast a glance in his direction. He now spends his time in the *service d'amour*, serving his lady humbly, without hope of reward, content only in his suffering and in his *amor purus*. Meanwhile he has confided in a friend or intermediary, hoping that he or she will be able to intercede with his lady and dispose her more favorably toward him. The lover also performs various great and noble deeds in the service of his lady, for it was thought that the practice of courtly love was an ennobling enterprise, productive of all virtue and all good. Next he becomes an *entendedor* (one whose love is tolerated). Eventually the lady returns his love, granting him the *bel acceuil* (the beautiful welcome). He is now a *drutz* (a full-fledged lover). The lovers now practice *fin'amors* (they may touch hands, kiss each other, and lie nude together), but they may not indulge in *amor mixtus* (sexual union) until the lover has proven the sincerity of his love.[111] Such is the outline of the general characteristics of courtly love, a "sickness" which elevates and depresses, causing both ecstasy and suffering, happiness and despair, filling the lover with courage, cowardice, and countless other conflicting emotions.[112]

---

[111] A.J. Denomy, *The Heresy of Courtly Love*, N.Y., 1947, speaks of the influences that the *sadilies* had on the development of *fin'amors,* a practice common among them long before the time of the troubadours.

[112] For further elaboration of the courtly conventions, see the chapter entitled "Courtly Love" in Otis H. Green, *Spain and the Western Tradition,* Univ. of Wisconsin Press, 1969, vol. I, pp. 72-126. The above paragraphs are a brief summary of this chapter.

Denis de Rougemont has chosen the myth of Tristan and Iseult as an example of the prototype of passionate love,[113] for the story gives him many good opportunities to elaborate on the nature of *erōs* (passionate love) as opposed to *agapē* (spiritual love). An important symbol in the myth is the love potion that causes Tristan and Iseult to fall in love with each other from the moment it touches their lips, making them the helpless slaves of a powerful force that is beyond their control but which is experienced by them as an emotion both pleasurable and painful in the extreme. These elements are found in the conventional presentation of *erōs* throughout modern European literature: "love at first sight," passivity and helplessness on the part of the lovers, possession of the lovers' spirit by a magical (or diabolical) force, and the inevitable blessed suffering. In contrast to *agapē*, *erōs* begins quickly and grips the lover with a surprising intensity. There is no need for him to know his beloved except in the most superficial way for, as de Rougemont points out,[114] he is in love with the idea of love, and not with the beloved. If the beloved returns his love, it is because she too is disposed to love in the same way and at the same time.

Passion, then, depends not so much on the virtues and qualities of the beloved as it does on the intensity of the imagination of the lover. To concentrate their imaginations on each other the lovers must be separated as much as possible. Passion is kept alive by finding obstacles to prevent their union, so marriage becomes the greatest enemy of *erōs,* for "whatever turns into a reality is no longer love."[115] The passionate lover must devote his energies to discovering new

---

[113] Denis de Rougemont, *Love in the Western World,* trans. M. Belgion, N.Y. 1940. (Fawcett edition, 1966) First published as *L'amour et L'Occident,* Paris, 1939.

[114] *Op. cit.,* see the chapter entitled "The Love of Love," pp. 39-44.

[115] De Rougemont, *op. cit.,* p. 36.

ways of preventing his desire from achieving satisfaction,
until finally he surrenders himself to his inevitable death.

These considerations help to describe the psychological
mechanisms involved in the development of passionate love,
but Lope, of course, was faced with the problem of putting
all this material into dramatic form. This he accomplished, as
we have seen time and again, by introducing various techniques of foreshadowing to allow the audience and the characters to know what was going to happen. One of the most
effective of these to appear in *El caballero de Olmedo* is the
fundamental, all-pervasive literary foreshadowing. The very
title of the play itself warns the audience that the action will
deal with a tragic subject, for everyone was well acquainted
with the words of the popular *copla* that could be heard on
almost any street corner:

> *Que de noche le mataron*
> *al caballero,*
> *la gala de Medina,*
> *la flor de Olmedo.*
> *Sombras le avisaron*
> *que no saliese,*
> *y le aconsejaron*
> *que no se fuese*
> *el caballero,*
> *la gala de Medina,*
> *la flor de Olmedo.*[116]

("They killed the knight in the dark of night—the pride of
Medina, the flower of Olmedo. Spirits warned him not to
leave, and they advised him not to go—the pride of Medina,
the flower of Olmedo.")

---

[116] For the origin and variations of the *copla*, see *El caballero de Olmedo*,
ed. Francisco Rico, Salamanca (Anaya), 1968, pp. 26-42 of the
introduction.

This short, simple *copla* contains all the basic elements of tragic irony: the material deals with a character of noble birth who is mysteriously murdered one night, even though he was warned ahead of time not to go to the place where danger awaited him. Irony is seen in the contrast between the knight's essential ignorance of the exact nature of his fate, and the superior knowledge of the ghosts, who can foresee that he is headed for doom. The tragedy of the ballad is that the knight is not entirely ignorant of what lies ahead, since after all he has been forewarned, and yet he cannot, or will not, do anything to avoid his fate. The rest of the play will elaborate the many intricate details of this tragic irony, as it slowly constructs a sort of pyramid of events which must eventually lead to the final, inevitable climax.

It is not only the *sombras,* of course, who have superior knowledge of what is in store for the hero. The spectators can also see farther and more clearly than Don Alonso, not only because they are acquainted with the ballad and its implications, but also because Don Alonso is playing the role of the passionate lover, by then so familiar to the audience through literary tradition. A great number of the spectators were avid readers of sentimental novels and books of chivalry, and those who were less well read had, to some extent, absorbed the notion of tragic love through various facets of poetic convention expressed in the theatre and especially in the poetry of the *cancioneros,* in which the concepts of passion, death, ecstasy, and suffering were constantly being mentioned. Thus the audience was already familiar with the passionate nature of Don Alonso's love and its mysterious connection with death and tragedy, so they were able to foresee his fate as step by step he brought himself nearer to his doom.[117]

---

[117] For the theme of passionate love in the poetry of the *cancioneros,* see Otis Green, "Courtly Love in the Spanish *Cancioneros" PMLA, LXIV,*

Don Alonso was created by Lope as a sort of Quixotic creature of poetic convention who unknowingly imitates literary models of passionate lovers. This necessarily makes him an ironic figure, for his words and behavior constantly describe the true meaning of his condition, even though he himself is at least initially ignorant. There is an excellent example of this kind of Sophoclean irony very early in the first act of *El caballero de Olmedo.* Don Alonso is telling Fabia about Doña Inés, "an angel of divine beauty" whom he had spotted at a fair on the previous day. He immediately felt an overwhelming desire for her, so he followed her into a chapel in order not to lose her from sight. He then recites the following *copla* to Fabia:

> *En una capilla entraron;*
> *yo, que siguiéndolas iba,*
> *entré imaginando bodas.*
> *¡Tanto quien ama imagina!*
> *Vime sentenciado a muerte,*
> *porque el amor me decía:*
> *"Mañana mueres, pues hoy*
> *te meten en la capilla."*

(Act I, Scene i)

("The [maidens] entered a chapel and I followed them inside, imagining wedding bells. That's how fanciful a lover can be! I saw myself sentenced to death, because love said to me: *Tomorrow you die, for today they have put you in the chapel* [to say your final prayers].")

1949, 247-301. For bibliographical material on this poetry, see especially the excellent introduction and notes by A. Rodríguez Moñino, *El Cancionero General* (Valencia, 1511; Anvers, 1573), *Noticias bibliográficas,* Madrid, 1958. See also Charles V. Aubrun, "Inventaire des sources pour l'étude de la poésie castillane du quinzième siècle," *Estudios dedicados a Menéndez Pidal,* Vol. IV, 1953, 297-330.

On the surface his words are based on the traditional poetic equation of love and death,[118] but the spectators see more than the protagonist can at this point, for they know that his speech is not just figurative but literally a prediction of things to come. They see him already in his role as passionate lover, for like his literary models, he has quickly contracted the disease of *hereos* and is now in the stage of *fenhedor.*[119] But the road of passionate love cannot lead to marriage, for marriage, as we have seen, necessarily brings about the death of passion, and so there emerges from this passage another ironic dilemma which is fundamental to the play. The sensitive reader or spectator will already be aware of the inescapable conflict between passion and marriage, so the irony of the words here is based on the contrast between what the characters expect in the way of happiness and fulfillment, and what we know is in store for them as lovers.[120]

---

[118] For further examples of the ironic situations that abound in the play, I refer the reader both to Rico's introduction to the Anaya edition, *op. cit.,* and also to his article "El caballero de Olmedo: amor , muerte, ironía," *Papeles de Son Armadans,* Oct. 1967, pp. 38-56, in which he gives a very extensive catalog of verbal ironies, especially those having to do with the equations "vida:amor; muerte:ausencia" (p.51).

[119] The title of the work and the play on words in this passage sets Don Alonso apart from the other more frivolous *galanes* in the Golden Age theatre, and this will be increasingly true as the various methods of foreshadowing prepare the audience for the tragic ending.

[120] William C. McCrary reprododuced a "romance" written in 1648 by Francisco de Borja on the subject of *El Caballero de Olmedo,* in which the poet chooses a married woman as the object of the *caballero*'s love (*The Goldfinch and the Hawk,* Chapel Hill, 1968, pp. 23-26). I would agree with McCrary that here "Borja is bold and Lope infinitely more subtle" (p. 27), and I would also add that the very fact that Inés is not married underscores the complexity of Don Alonso's predicament by making us conscious that there is a conflict between passion and marriage. Had Inés been married, we would not have had to question his motives in trying to remain separated from her.

It becomes clear at this point that one of the first consequences of Don Alonso's surrender to passion is his newly
heightened capacity for self-deception. Thus he soon convinces himself that he wants to marry Inés, yet never once
during the play does he take a decisive step toward bringing
this about. His reticence, however, is very understandable in
the light of what has already been said about the nature of
passion: he pretends to be courting Inés, yet underneath it all
he is really courting death. The tragedy of Don Alonso is that
he cannot, and will not, do otherwise.

Doña Inés is a tacit collaborator in the game of passion,
for she is equally willing to cast about for excuses not to
marry Alonso. At first she shows an interest in marrying him
soon after she admits to Leonor that she is attracted to him.
Later on Fabia hastens to assure Inés that Alonso's intentions
are honorable and that he plans to marry her, but by this time
she has started to feel hesitant about the matter. If she had
been like the average lady of her day, she would have subtly
but firmly pursued a course of action leading as directly as
possible to marriage, a goal that would have put Don Alonso
in an embarrassing position. Instead, she cooperates with
him in setting up obstacles to their union:

> Pero, ¡triste!, ¿cómo puedo
> ser suya, si a don Rodrigo
> me da mi padre don Pedro?   (I, vv. 873-876)

("But poor me! How can I be his if my father, Don Pedro,
has promised me to Don Rodrigo?")

Although this flimsy excuse is a common technique
used in Golden Age plays to add further problems to the love
entanglement, it acquires a special meaning here for it reflects the fundamental attitude of Doña Inés in her role as the
traditional lady in the courtly game of love. She, like Don
Alonso, believes that what she really wants is a peaceful,
lasting relationship with her lover, when the truth is that as

long as her passion remains unchanged it is at cross purposes with marriage. Both Alonso and Inés wear the mask of conventional lovers whose goal is conjugal love, but behind the masks are the faces of passionate lovers whose actions are controlled by the need for obstacles and separation.

While the lovers are bent on hiding the true nature of their passion, Lope betrays them by unmasking them to the audience. From the beginning of the first act he makes it clear to the spectators that the lovers' passion is doomed. A significant piece of foreshadowing occurs when Don Alonso tells Fabia that he "heard" Inés say to him with her eyes:

> *No os vais, don Alonso, a Olmedo,*
> *quedaos agora en Medina.*   (I, vv. 133-134)

("Don't go, Don Alonso, to Olmedo. Stay now in Medina.")

This entreaty is understood by Don Alonso to be nothing more than a much desired and very exciting invitation whose effect is to fortify passion through hope. But for the audience and the reader, the effect is entirely different. The entreaty becomes a warning, and the warning is the foreshadowing of doom, for both audience and reader are familiar with the words of the *copla,* which will continue to be repeated like tolling bells during the rest of the play. From this point on the comic quality of the first two acts carries with it the ever-present shadow of tragedy, a tragedy which grows stronger as the action unfolds. Now that the audience has been made aware, the light-hearted banter of the characters acquires an ominous tone, and the spectators watch in fascination as Alonso fulfills every prophecy of misfortune, one by one. The members of the audience are in the privileged position of sharing with the author a "God-like" view of the action, now that they know that Don Alonso is heading for disaster. We have here a perfect example of the ironic relationship of audience and protagonist: the spectators, unaffected by the blindness of passion, can see the dangers that Don Alonso refuses to acknowledge. They are aware of both the masks of self-deception and the faces of the lovers underneath, so they are able to listen ironically to Don Alonso as he continues to deceive himself about Fabia's character, the perfection of Inés, and the hope of enjoying fulfillment where none can be found.

We have seen how the repetitious mention of the towns of Olmedo and Medina during the first two acts alerted the audience to the future tragedy because of their acquaintance with the words of the popular *copla*. Lope used another type of literary foreshadowing to elicit from the audience similar feelings of foreboding when he introduced Fabia into the play at the beginning of Act I, for we are all aware of the role that Celestina played in the lives and subsequent deaths of Calixto and Melibea. McCrary has done an admirable job of analyzing the ominous feeling that emanates from Fabia as she practices the various forms of her witchcraft,[121] and there is no doubt that her presence helps to prepare the spectators for the tragic ending.[122] The other fundamental aspect of Fabia's character, her bawdy comicity, has been described by Bataillon as "un hommage de Lope au génie comique de Rojas,"[123] and he emphasizes her importance as a figure of comic relief. But it should be particularly stressed here that the humor of the first two acts makes a significant contribution to the overall dramatic irony of the play. Now that the

---

[121] *The Goldfinch and the Hawk;* see the chapter entitled "Alcahuetería and Brujería," pp. 51-82. For further particulars concerning the figure of the bawd, see Michael J. Ruggerio, "The Evolution of the Go-Between in Spanish Literature Through the Sixteenth Century, " Univ. of California Publications in Modern Philology, 78, 1966.
[122] Frank Casa, "The Dramatic Unity of *El caballero de Olmedo, " Neo-philologus,* L, 1966, 234-243. See especially pp, 240-242.
[123] Marcel Bataillon, *La Célestine selon Fernando de Rojas,* Paris, 1961, p. 250.

spectators foresee the inevitable outcome of Don Alonso's love, they cannot help but sense the contradictions inherent in each one of these comic episodes, which will eventually be interlaced with the tragic irony of the final act. We have noted how Don Alonso's exaggerated praise of Fabia is both humorous and painful to the spectators, who know that he is deceiving himself. To this example could be added many more, but for the sake of brevity I shall mention only the witty scene in which Tello and Fabia pretend to be Latin tutor and *religiosa,* respectively,[124] for not only does the discrepancy between the appearance and the reality of the role-players' identity lend a humorous and ironic touch to the play within the play, but it is also ironic that Doña Inés, who hypocritically asks her father to let her enter a monastery, will end up making the same request in earnest during the last scene of the play. A.A. Parker's words sum up this observation: "The comic element itself fuses with the tragedy by heightening its irony, for the comedy is the sign of the impetuous overconfidence of the lovers in the pursuit of a happiness whose graves they are themselves digging."[125]

Our positions differ, however, when it comes to suggesting an explanation as to why the lovers are digging a grave for their happiness. Parker feels that Alonso's death comes as a punishment for his having solicited the services of a disreputable bawd,[126] but it should be noted that Lope used a Celestina-like figure in several other plays, without the protagonists incurring any punishment by way of poetic justice.[127] Instead, it has already been shown previously that

---

[124] Such parodies are not uncommon in the Golden Age theatre; similar scenes appear in Tirso's *Marta la piadosa* and in Lope's *Dómine Lucas.*
[125] A.A. Parker, "The Approach to the Spanish Drama of the Golden Age," *The Tulane Drama Review,* IV, 1959, 42-59. Quote on p. 48.
[126] *Op. cit.,* p. 47.
[127] The best examples of these are *La bella malmaridada, El amante agradecido,* and *El rufián Castrucho,* but none of these plays has an

Alonso's death is connected with the nature and meaning of passion, and with the fact that the truly passionate lover uses the game not as a means to an end, but as an end in itself. When passion takes precedence over life, when a player is willing to sacrifice everything to keep his passion alive, then he must inevitably give up his personal freedom. Instead of using the game to his own advantage, he must become a helpless pawn whose function is to live as long as possible within the limits of the rules. Once the game starts drawing to a close, the existence of the pawn is seriously threatened and he must find new ways of extending the game, or he has to resign. But resignation is unendurable to one who depends on the game to give meaning to his life, so Don Alonso begins to concentrate his efforts on the search for what might be described as "extension devices."

It was not long before Fabia emerged as the character best suited for this purpose, and it soon becomes clear that her function is ironical in an unexpected way, for while it appears quite evident that her services will endanger Don Alonso's chances of marrying Doña Inés, it turns out that she is actually playing right into his hands. Although he insists that his only goal is marriage, the old bawd is not a servant of *agapē* but of *erōs,* so in eliciting her help, Don Alonso's actions belie his words.

Fabia naturally becomes an ideal counselor for the two lovers. She is a connoisseur of passion, she is knowledgeable about the rules of the game, and she is relentless in her ap-

---

unhappy ending; the worst so-called punishment involves tricking the unsuspecting lover into seducing the old bawd who has cleverly availed herself of the damsel's bed. The influence of *La Celestina* in such plays as *El arenal de Sevilla, El anzuelo de Fenisa,* or *La francesilla* is so minimal that it does not really have any bearing on the subject. For a complete analysis of the figure of La Celestina in Lope's *Comedia,* see Edward Nagy, *Lope de Vega y "La Celestina,"* Mexico (Univ. Vera-cruzana), 1968.

plication of them to her young clients. She knows that in order to keep their excitement at a high pitch she must make sure they always move from one emotional extreme to the other, never resting too long with either certainty or despair. Thus she cleverly allows Inés to suspect that the anonymous bachelor who wrote the letter is Don Alonso, but she never permits her to relax in the absolute assurance that this is so (I, vv. 373-396).

Fabia applies the same tactics to Don Alonso when she goes to his house to report on the afternoon's proceedings. When she claims to have been beaten for her trouble by some of Inés's lackeys, Don Alonso immediately succumbs to despair, believing that his lady is angry with him.[128] But she quickly rescues him from his torment by presenting him with Inés's reply to his letter, and within the blink of an eye his passion returns with twice the force it had before. Wonder-struck and lost in amazement, he turns to his servant and says "*Hinca, Tello, la rodilla.*" ("Bend, Tello, your knee." Act I, v. 567), leaving us with another example of ironically painful comicity. The roots of his passion are deeper than ever now that he "lost" and then "regained" Inés through Fabia's trickery. There is a parallel reaction on Inés's part when she is deceived by the episode of the green ribbon into thinking that Alonso does not love her (I, 743-750), but then Fabia comes along and tells her that it was indeed Don Alonso, and none other, who sent her the love letter. Inés feels so elated and comforted by this information that she breaks down and confesses everything to the exultant Fabia, who knows that her fear of having lost Don Alonso and her

---

[128] Cf. Capellanus, *op. cit.*, p. 27: "Love increases, too, if one of the lovers shows that he is angry at the other; for the lover falls at once into a great fear that this feelng which has arisen in his beloved may last forever."

relief at getting him back have finally crystallized[129] her passion. Fabia, it must be conceded, has won the day.

It has generally been thought that Fabia's services were not needed, since there were no real obstacles to prevent Don Alonso from marrying Doña Inés.[130] Both Bataillon and Rico contend that she was introduced by Lope for the purpose of amusing the audience, Parker suggests that Lope used her to lay the groundwork for Don Alonso's punishment in the end, McCrary connects her role with the heretical aspects of courtly love, and Casa feels that her presence serves as a device for lengthening the otherwise undramatic action of the first two acts, as well as lending unity to the play as a whole. Yet while all these positions are perfectly valid, one should not overlook the irony of Fabia's function as an "extension device" to keep the lovers' passion alive, for although the traditional intermediary was used to help the lover surmount the obstacles which lay in his path, Fabia provides Don Alonso with the hope, fear, and excitement necessary to prolong this stage of passionate love as much as possible.

The figure of Don Rodrigo would also present a perplex-ing problem were it not for what has already been said about the paradoxes of passion, for it is clear that he offers no real obstacle to the lovers since Inés does not love him and Don Pedro would have had no objections to her marrying Don Alonso (III, vv. 745-751). Obviously Don Rodrigo serves the dramatic purpose of adding superficial conflict to the lovers' relationship, and he ultimately becomes the necessary instru-

---

[129] It was Marcel Proust, a brilliant connoisseur of passionate love, who coined this word to describe a similar approach to increasing passionate love in *A la recherche du temps perdu.*

[130] Unlike Melibea, Inés had no need to be convinced by Fabia to love Alonso, for her passion was already strong before Fabia ever set foot in her house (215-245).

ment of Don Alonso's death, but he also shares Fabia's function in increasing their passion.[131] During the first two acts we are constantly aware of the theme of death in the words of the ballad which Tello repeats as he warns Alonso that his many trips between Olmedo and Medina[132] are beginning to make it hard for him to keep his love a secret.[133] But Alonso is undaunted by the warning, claiming he owes it to Inés to surmount this small hardship for her sake, especially since he has even less to overcome than Leandro, who swam the Hellespont every night in order to be with his lady. Tello is quick to point out the ending of that tragic tale, explaining that in this case the danger is not the rough sea but rather the jealous Rodrigo, who has taken note of his frequent trips between Olmedo and Medina and has deduced their meaning (II, vv. 61-66).

Both the reader and the audience, as usual, sense the ominous nature of Rodrigo's jealousy, but for Don Alonso it only acts as a catalyst. Up to this moment the lovers manage to keep their excitement at a high level with the help of Fabia and the self-imposed separations they are forced to endure. But temporary separation and small obstacles are not enough to keep passion alive; what is needed is extravagant, unequivocal danger. This danger, as far as Don Alonso is concerned has materialized itself in the person of Don Rodrigo, who threatens not only to put an end to his life, but also to separate him permanently from his beloved. Soon after learning

---

[131] Cf. Capellanus, *op. cit.,* p. 27: "So, too, if you know that someone is trying to win your beloved away from you, that will no doubt increase your love and you will begin to feel more affection for her."

[132] Capellanus, p. 27: "When you have gone to some other place or are about to go away—that increases your love."

[133] Rule XIII as cited by Capellanus: "When made public, love rarely endures" (p.42), and again: "Lovers should not even nod to each other unless they are sure that nobody is watching them" (p. 25).

of his rival's intention to marry Inés, Don Alonso delivers
his most impassioned speech:

> Inés me quiere, yo adoro
> a Inés, yo vivo en Inés;
> todo lo que Inés no es
> desprecio, aborrezco, ignoro.
> Inés es mi bien, yo soy
> esclavo de Inés; de Olmedo
> a Medina vengo y voy,
>   porque Inés mi dueña es
> para vivir o morir.   (II, vv. 101-110)

("Inés loves me, and I adore Inés, I live for Inés; I scorn,
hate, and disregard anything that is not Inés. Inés means
everything to me; I am her slave. From Olmedo to Medina I
come and go, because Inés is my lady in life and in death.")

Again the mention of the ballad towns, again the foreboding, and once more an example of how passion, at the
very peak of its intensity, is so closely associated with the
concept of death. It is as if an individual's entire life could be
exchanged for one glorious, unique moment of ecstasy. In a
strictly dramatic sense, of course, death is almost inevitable
after such an unparalleled high point, for any other alternative would be anticlimactic. But Don Alonso, although he is
a character in a play which we know must terminate with a
dramatic flourish, is by his very nature an advocate of the
bang and not the whimper. He senses that his own life is a
dramatic unity that could never admit an anticlimax, so he
puts everything—life, passion, ecstasy, death—into the
balance.

The jocular spirit of the second act is a form of irony in
itself, as we contrast Fabia's and Tello's unabashed glee with
Alonso's habitual melancholia. The closer he gets to con-
ceiving of the possibility of possessing Inés, however, the

more troubled he becomes. Don Alonso is to the *cancioneros* what Don Quixote is to the *Amadís;* he has interiorized the role of the courtly lover, and plays his part to the hilt. Like his literary counterparts, Don Alonso discovers that absence brings him face-to-face with a perplexing conflict: the suffering it causes him intensifies his melancholia, while at the same time it quickens his desire. Inés's presence, one must assume, would do just the opposite: the relief would revivify his spirits, while at the same time it would kill his desire.

The dilemma seems hopeless. Part of him must live at the expense of the other no matter what course of action he takes. For the first time Don Alonso sees death as a sort of welcome salvation, a unique and enticing remedy for his unavoidable conflict. From this time on he actively courts his fate, rather than passively accepting it as something that he is unable to control.

Until this point both Alonso and Inés had been in collaboration with each other to extend the game by setting up obstacles to their marriage, as we have seen from the way they made use of Fabia and Rodrigo. Now, however, Alonso faces a new crisis when Inés unexpectedly invites him to make love to her, for he senses that this union would be as much of a threat to them as marriage itself. He refuses her invitation, but not without presenting himself and the spectators with an elaborate explanation of his decision:

> Cuando mi amor no fuera
> de fe tan pura y limpia,
> las perlas de sus ojos
> mi muerte solicitan.
> Llorando por mi ausencia
> Inés quedó aquel día,
> que sus lágrimas fueron
> de sus palabras firma.
> Bien sabe aquella noche
> que pudiera ser mía.

Cobarde amor, ¿qué aguardas,
cuando respetos miras?
¡Ay, Dios, qué gran desdicha,
partir el alma y dividir la vida!

                                          (II, vv. 757-760)

("If my love were not based on such a pure, unsullied faith,
her opalescent eyes would be the death of me. I left Inés
weeping that day because I had to go away; her tears proved
her words [her declaration of love] to be true. Well she knew
that she could be mine that night. Cowardly love, what are
you waiting for? Why do you let respect hold you back? Oh,
God! What a great misfortune it is to have to cut one's soul
in half and divide one's life in two!")

Like many another courtly lover, Don Alonso has idealized
his lady and wishes to keep her standing forever pure and
unavailable on her pedestal, preferring *amor purus* to *amor
mixtus*. But Inés is not always as cooperative as she might be
on this particular score, for in offering to step down from her
pedestal she is putting her lover in the awkward position of
having to find new obstacles to place between them; it is the
purity of his love and his respect for Inés's honor that now
become the reason for their continued separation. One cannot
help but conclude that he is exploiting the chivalric code for
his own purposes, using it as yet another "extension device"
to protect his passion which is now being threatened with
satisfaction.

     Don Alonso clearly sees the danger of her invitation as
once again he mentions his own death: *las perlas de sus ojos
mi muerte solicitan*. To yield to Inés is to destroy the one
thing he values more highly than life itself, yet to ignore her
tears and to resist the temptation of accepting the joy she
offers to share with him takes almost superhuman control, a
control which must *partir el alma y dividir la vida*. It is
extremely difficult for Don Alonso to extend the period of

precador (one who pleads his case) when Doña Inés declines the role of *la belle dame sans merci* (the beautiful but unmerciful lady). The end of the game is drawing near. The insoluble nature of his dilemma has been carefully established throughout the second act. Fearing the emptiness of a life without Inés, Don Alonso rejects Tello's advice to deny his passion before it is too late; fearing the letdown of an anti-climax, he decides not to kill his desire through satisfaction; worried that his passion might die of its own accord, he seeks to rekindle it with obstacles and danger. He finds himself surrounded by locked doors, unable to undertake any action that could obviate or mitigate his tragic destiny.

We have seen that the first two acts differed radically from the third act both in tone and spirit, and it has also been noted that the jocularity of the first and second acts strikes an ironic contrast with the somber final act. There is yet another basic difference between these two major parts of the play, however, and this involves the specific techniques of foreshadowing that Lope uses. It is a curious fact that every one of the devices of supernatural foreshadowing (as opposed to literary foreshadowing) with which we have become familiar appears in the last scene of Act Two. Only then does Lope use these more obvious devices of foreshadowing, beginning with the episode of the goldfinch and the hawk, then going on to the scene with the silent *sombra* and, finally, the song of the mysterious *labrador* (farmer). This, of course, could be partially explained by the nature of Act One, which makes it difficult to introduce any devices of foreshadowing that would actually overpower the general spirit of levity that Lope has introduced at this point. It could, perhaps, also be explained in terms of dramatic expediency, for the intensity and force of these devices must necessarily increase as the climax approaches.

If we examine this phenomenon in light of what we already know about Don Alonso and his role as passionate lover, however, we find that the new devices of foreshadowing indicate a subtle change of emphasis: whereas in the beginning of the play the major conflict concerned his struggle against the threat of the death of passion, the action now centers itself around the tragic nature of his own inevitable destiny. We have seen that Don Alonso began to accept the idea of death with a certain resignation, perhaps even with a modicum of relief; but now he is always being warned by supernatural forces to avoid taking steps that might lead to his doom.

It becomes evident that his conflict has shifted from the vain struggle to cope with the paradoxes of passion to the broader, more philosophical problem of dealing with the conflicting demands of desire and reason, of the death wish and the life force. Don Alonso's reason, or life force, or better judgment are all reflected in the warnings expressed by the devices of foreshadowing, devices that are best understood as facets of his own nature which act as a counterforce to his growing resignation to his forthcoming death. The stronger his resignation, the more urgent the warnings that attempt to penetrate his melancholy renunciation of life. It now ceases to be a question of how to prevent passion from dying; it has become a question of choosing between passion and life. But we know, as does Don Alonso too, that there is really no choice to be made.

The first piece of specific foreshadowing occurs in the last scene of the second act when Don Alonso informs Tello that he has been greatly disturbed by a horrible scene he witnessed from his window at dawn: there in his garden he saw a hawk swoop down and kill a little goldfinch, while his mate looked on helplessly. Don Alonso was depressed by the obvious symbolism of this event in much the same way that Queen Etelfrida had been worried about her falcon's having been killed by an *ave ratera* (a bird of prey that flies close to the ground in search of mice and small birds or animals). In both cases the episode involved foreshadowing that was very clear to the spectators, even though the characters themselves could only sense a sort of vague foreboding.[134] In both cases too, we witness an ironic interplay between the character who is disturbed by the prophetic incident and the skeptical character who either misinterprets its meaning or firmly denies that it has any meaning at all. Thus Tello chides Don Alonso for seeing what he thought was an ominous message in the death of the goldfinch:

> Tello: *Ven a Medina, y no hagas*
> *caso de sueños ni agüeros,*
> *cosas a la fe contrarias.* (II, vv. 918-920)

("Come to Medina, and pay no attention to dreams or omens, which are contrary to the faith.")

Once again the "clairvoyant" character decides to disregard what he calls his *revelaciones del alma* ("the revelations of his soul," II, 876) because he is afraid that paying credence to omens goes against the decrees of the Church. The irony of this fear has already been mentioned on several occasions, when it was pointed out that if the protagonist had been less anxious to be a good Christian, he might have been able to avoid falling into the trap that awaited him. What is even more ironic in the case of passionate lovers is the fact that the very nature of their amorous passion is incompatible with Church doctrine, and yet they insist on scrupulously

---

[134] McCrary (*The Goldfinch and the Hawk*, pp. 113-123) attributes Don Alonso's prophetic dream to a love-sickness described in the Golden Age as "melancholic adustion." The lover's rational faculty would be disturbed by the superabundance of heat generated by his passion, his imagination would be unduly excited, and as a result he would often become clairvoyant. Although we have seen in the course of this study many cases of clairvoyance that were not caused by amorous passion, the symptoms of this "disease" are nevertheless pertinent to the analysis of *El caballero de Olmedo* in that they confirm what has already been said about the conflict of passion and reason.

observing the finer and more superficial rules of orthodoxy. Don Alonso, like his many dramatic counterparts, turns a deaf ear to the *avisos del alma* (the warnings of his soul, II v. 908) in spite of his better judgment, convincing himself that by disregarding these *avisos* and *revelaciones* he is fulfilling his duty to the Church. The irony of his self-deception is evident to the spectators, who have ample opportunity during the first two acts to foresee the consequences of his actions, but what lends special depth to the tragedy is the fact that Don Alonso himself is aware of his own self-deception, and yet he is unable or unwilling to renounce the passion which has become more important to him than life itself.

His knowledge and fatalistic acceptance of his looming death is nowhere so evident as in his parting speech to Inés, just before he leaves for Olmedo with the ironic intention of reassuring his parents that he is not dead but alive. The entire farewell is reminiscent of the paradoxical sentiments in the poetry of the *cancionero,* which so admirably reflects the age-old conflicts felt by passionate lovers through the years. The lover is caught between the desire for the presence of his beloved and the inevitability of her necessary absence—between the ecstasy and the suffering inspired by his passion, between the need to live for his love and the consciousness of approaching death. This unequivocal knowledge of death is subtly interwoven into the main body of the speech by the interspersion of the well-known *coplas antiguas* that were used by Cervantes in his preface to *Persiles y Segismunda:*

> *Puesto ya el pie en el estribo,*
> *con las ansias de la muerte,*
> *Señora, aquesta te escribo...*

("With my foot already in the stirrup [having mounted the legendary horse of Moorish tradition that will carry him to heaven], and feeling the anxieties of death, my lady, this I write to you...")

But when Inés objects to his pessimistic certainty that they will soon be forever parted, Alonso again falls back on his well-established pattern of disregarding the warning signs that plague him, reassuring her that

> han sido
> estas imaginaciones
> sólo un ejercicio triste
> del alma, que me atormenta.   (III, 420-423)
>
> de sueños y fantasías
> si bien falsas ilusiones
> han nacido estas razones.   (III, 426-428)

("these imaginings were only the pathetic promptings of my tormented soul... my thoughts sprang from dreams and fantasies, even though they were false illusions.")

Don Alonso denies what he knows to be true, while at the same time his knowledge of the truth prevents him from believing his denial, as evidenced by his parting statement:

> Aquí se acabó mi vida,
> que es lo mismo que partirme   (III, 438-439)

("My life has ended here, which is the same thing as cutting myself in two.")

The *avisos del alma* (the warnings of the soul) have now grown louder than ever as Don Alonso continues to do what he can to ignore them, responding with increasingly self-deceptive rationalizations born of his need to preserve his amorous passion at all costs.

During the course of this series of escalating warnings and their accompanying rationalizations put forth by Don Alonso, a dramatic moment occurs after his farewell speech when he is about to set out alone on the road to Olmedo. As he crosses the stage he is suddenly confronted by a *sombra*

with his hand on his sword, wearing a hat and a black mask.
Don Alonso reacts with understandable shock and terror:

> *Alonso: ¿Qué es esto? ¿Quién va? De oírme*
> *no hace caso. ¿Quién es? Hable.*
> *¡Que un hombre me atemorice*
> *no habiendo temido a tantos!*
> *¿Es don Rodrigo? ¿No dice quién es?*

("What is this? Who goes there? He's paying no attention to
what I'm saying. Who is it? Speak up! Imagine my being
terrorized by a man, when so many others have failed to
scare me! Is he Don Rodrigo? Won't you tell me who you
are?")

This *sombra* seems to be an extension of Don Alonso's
own *persona*, a sort of recriminatory superego that appears,
as in the case of the Romantic *Doppelgänger,* in moments of
extreme emotional stress. Don Alonso's inner conflict was
brought to a climax by the chain of events immediately preceding his supernatural experience, and he reacts to the
sombra in much the same way as the other passionate lovers.
At first he is frightened by the specter, burdened as he is with
an uneasy conscience, then he challenges it in a fit of jittery
bravado. Finally, after the *sombra* leaves, he comes up with a
number of rationalizations to explain the ghost's appearance,
for he is determined not to accept it as an omen of the tragic
fate he knows is in store for him. His rationalizations are all
echoes of similar ones presented by the skeptical characters
in other plays: first he offers himself an explanation based on
a purely logical interpretation of what he thought might be a
natural phenomenon: he tells himself that the *sombra* was
merely his own shadow. This explanation quickly disproves
itself when the ghost has speaks aloud, so Don Alonso thinks
his depressed imagination is playing tricks on him. The
danger of this explanation is that it is partially correct, but it
fails to penetrate the meaning of his experience deeply

enough. Instead of dwelling on this possibility, however, Don Alonso chides himself for being fearful for no apparent reason, which makes him feel ashamed of what he considers to be appropriate only for *sujetos humildes* (lowly folks). It now becomes a matter of honor, for a knight should never be cowardly in the face of danger, so this now emerges as yet another reason for rejecting the experience. Finally, it occurs to him that the *sombra* must be one of Fabia's magic tricks which was intended to warn him to be wary of envy. This hypothesis is also dangerous in that it is partially true, for envy will certainly inspire the instrument of his death. But what Don Alonso's explanations fail to take into account is the fact that he himself is the worker of his own downfall, for his passion has caused him to become deaf to the *avisos del alma* (the soul's warnings), embodied in the *sombra.*

Our examination of the function and meaning of the silent *sombras* leads us to question McCrary's interpretation of the role of Don Alonso's ghost, which he believes is a diabolical vision conjured up by Fabia for the purpose of "bringing about the death of the young knight."[135] To prove his theory that the specter was the work of Satan, McCrary quotes excerpts from Golden Age authorities that describe the nature of demonic visions, many of which have certain qualities in common with Lope de Vega's *sombras:* "the demon's presence is known by the terrifying emotional impact it produces, whereas God's voice produces a feeling of calm and inner tranquility" (p. 145); "the black attire, especially the black mask, would indicate that the *Fénix* (Lope) intended for this phantom to represent a demoniacal phenomenon" (p. 146); what is more, "evil spirits were believed more likely to appear at night," and they also showed up on crossroads: "metaphorically Don Alonso has arrived at the crossroad of decision" (p. 147).

---

[135] McCrary, *Goldfinch,* pp. 143-151. Quote on p. 149.

But it has already been pointed out that the characters who saw the *sombras* were terrified because their uneasy consciences were warning them about the potentially fatal outcome of their love; and if the specters were dressed in black, it was a dramatically and visually powerful symbol of doom and looming death. As for their appearing at night and at crossroads, this was not a requisite for the *sombras* in any other plays that we have studied, although the midnight hour certainly heightens the romantic and ominous effect. There can be no doubt that their purpose was to warn the lover of the dangers ahead, and to do everything possible to *deter* him from pursuing a path that would lead to certain disaster.

Hearkening back to *El robo de Dina,* we remember that when Siquén, driven by his passion for Dina, attempts to violate her for the second time, the *sombra* prevents him from entering her rooms (p. 106 above). Siquén was badly frightened by what he correctly interpreted as an omen of his death, as was Jelando when a specter dressed in black tried to warn him of his own sad fate (p. 110-111 above). King Alfonso is also confronted by a *sombra* who prevents him from joining Raquel (p.118 above), but the King realizes that the supernatural phenomena are heavenly messages:

> *...parece que la voz dijo*
> *que de aqueste atrevimiento*
> *estaba el Cielo ofendido."*

("It appears that the voice said Heaven was offended by that audacity." See p. 122 above.)

Otón comes to the same conclusion when he says that God is punishing him, and Ataúlfo advises him not to disregard the warning:

> *"Señor, si el cielo dices que te avisa*
> *No vayas contra el cielo."* (compare p. 137 above)

("Sir, if you say heaven is warning you, do not pit yourself against heaven.")

Even Don Alonso himself admits, after he has been mortally wounded, that he paid too little attention to the *avisos del cielo* ("heavenly warnings") *Acad. III*, pp. 651-652.

Granted, then, that the *sombras* are manifestations of God's will reflected in the conscience or the better judgment or the higher nature of the passionate lover, it now becomes difficult to agree with McCrary's hypothesis that Fabia is a servant of the Devil, bent on bringing about Don Alonso's perdition, for she is evidently joining forces with the *avisos del cielo* to warn him of his approaching death. One should not necessarily take too literally Don Alonso's suggestion that the *sombra* was conjured up by Fabia, for in the first place the specters in the other plays were quite capable of materializing without any help from bawds or witches, and secondly, Don Alonso wanted to find an excuse to convince himself that the *sombra* was merely a piece of trickery so that he could then more easily ignore its warning. Alonso deceived himself in exactly the same way:

> *Vive el Cielo que lo entiendo,*
> *y que todos son hechizos*
> *de Leonor, para quitarme*
> *el gusto que emprendo y sigo!* (cf. p. 122 above)

("By Heaven I know what is going on now! Leonor is practicing her witchcraft on me to keep me from enjoying the pleasure that I strive for and pursue!")

Whether Fabia was behind the *sombra* incident or not, it is abundantly clear that she is trying to warn Don Alonso by means of the famous *copla* sung by the *labrador* (farmer) who claims to have learned it from her a short while before. Fabia must have specifically instructed him to find Don

Alonso and sing him the verses, for after he has finished, the *labrador* tells him:

> *Si os importa, ya cumplí*
> *con deciros la canción.*
> *Volved atrás; no paséis*
> *deste arroyo.*   (*Acad.* III. pp. 593-596)

("If it matters to you, I have now fulfilled my obligation by reciting the verses. Turn back, do not cross this stream.")

According to McCrary's thesis, then, the good peasant must have been a messenger of the Devil's disciple. But if Fabia wished to bring about Don Alonso's demise in order to "blaspheme the Maker and demonstrate Satan's reality," (McCrary, p. 150), why then would she take so much trouble to forewarn Don Alonso of his fate? McCrary suggests that Fabia's plan is to deceive the knight with the truth, quoting Lavater[136] as saying (in modernized English): "The Devil sometimes utters the truth so that his words may have more credit, and so he may more easily beguile" (p. 150).

This is not a particularly good example, however, of "*el engaño con la verdad*" (using the truth to deceive). If the Devil (Fabia) sometimes utters the truth (passion leads to death), when and how does this help her to beguile Don Alonso? The fact is that Don Alonso deceives *himself,* and has been doing so ever since the onset of his "melancholic adustion" (see p. 203, n. 53) or *hereōs* (the yearning and burning madness associated with passionate love) which has excited his senses and clouded his reason. McCrary says that "Fabia knows that once Alonso commits himself to the dance of love he cannot turn back" (p.150); from which one infers

---

[136] Lewes Lavater, *Of Ghostes and Spirites Walking by Nyght.* Translated by R. H. London, 1572. Facsimile ed. By J. Dover Wilson and May Yardley. Oxford, England, 1929. Quote on p. 173.)

that she is not worried about losing her victim even if she does forewarn him, but this still does not clarify what her exact motivation would be and where the deception lies, assuming she does represent the Devil.

Finally McCrary hits on the real purpose of this scene when he says that Lope "underlines dramatically just how blind Alonso is at this time" (p. 151), but to accomplish this, Fabia does not need to be the Devil's disciple. The fact that Alonso cannot heed the benevolent *voces del cielo* (heavenly voices) which coincide with his own *revelaciones del alma* (revelations of the soul) is more poignant and tragic than if he were simply to disregard the devilish machinations of one who might have attempted to "deceive him with the truth."

Fabia is no angel, but in spite of her dabblings in black magic, it is perhaps a bit extreme to equate her with Satan. She follows the traditional pattern of the old go-between who enjoys the vicarious pleasure she gets from reliving her own lusty younger days through the passionate experiences of her clients, while lining her pockets with the revenue from her dubious activities. She knows how to foster passion, how to encourage it and make it reach great heights, but it is doubtful that she wishes to bring her clients to ruin and perdition. Perhaps the majority of the lovers she dealt with knew how to play the game in a spirit of levity, as they did in those plays in which her counterparts gleefully went about their work with only the most humorous consequences (see p. 151 above, footnote 125), but Don Alonso's sensitive soul was probably beyond her comprehension.

When Fabia finally realizes that his passion is too strong and too deep to allow him to continue playing a game that requires a certain frivolity and cynicism if one is to avoid perishing in the flames, it is already too late. She tries to warn him through the poetic medium best suited to his own spirit, and she succeeds to the point of causing him severe depression and terror, but he is so completely committed to his passion that he cannot turn back. If there is any devil to be found in this tragic drama, it is hidden somewhere in the very nature of passion itself, which ironically claims as its victims only the noblest lovers. That Fabia was partly responsible for fostering this fatal passion in Don Alonso and Doña Inés is undeniable, but in the last analysis she is really no more culpable than Juliet's nurse. The tragedy of the play lies in the fact that Don Alonso, like all the passionate lovers we have examined so far, foresaw the fatal consequences of his passion and yet was unable or unwilling to take any action that would have obviated his tragic fate.

Conclusion

All the protagonists in the plays examined in this book are warned by means of various devices of fore-shadowing what the future has in store for them. When the prophecies promise them a fortunate destiny as they do, for example, in *La hermosa Éster*, *Los trabajos de Jacob*, or *El mejor mozo de España*, the characters can confidently undertake whatever action is necessary to attain their goals without feeling inner conflict or self-doubt. Even though the spectators are able to foresee the outcome just as clearly as the characters themselves, Lope nevertheless holds the attention of the spectators by presenting heroic figures with whom they can identify and for whom they may cheer. They are amused and delighted by other theatrical contrivances too, such as the battles, pageantry, dances, and stage machinery that Lope handles with such unusual originality and skill.

If Lope uses devices of foreshadowing to heighten the audience's expectations about the destinies of their favorite heroes, he also uses such devices to excite their hatred of despised villains. A perfect example of this can be found in *El último godo*, when Don Rodrigo's obvious misinterpretations of the bad omens must have made the spectators hiss and boo at the foolish, self-deceptive villain. They know what will befall him, and they relish the moment when he will be punished just as they enjoy his apparent ignorance of what lies ahead.

The devices of foreshadowing are used not only to let the audience gloat over the future of evil characters, but also to evoke pity for the fate of the innocent victim. Valdovinos, the noble suitor in *El marqués de Mantua,* is an excellent example of this type of character. Although he is forewarned of a future danger by some bad omens, he refuses to believe what they imply. The audience, on the other hand, is fully aware of what awaits him, and they must watch helplessly as he innocently places his trust in his treacherous so-called friend who ends up murdering him. In the cases of heroes, villains, and innocent victims, then, Lope uses devices of foreshadowing to evoke various emotional responses from his audience: pride in the destinies of heroes, cruel pleasure in the future punishments of villains, and sentimental pity for the victims of an unjust fate.

Lope's talent for manipulating the emotions of his audience was partially responsible for his great popularity, but the protagonists of his better plays are not patterned along the lines of the more prosaic heroes, villains, and victims. These protagonists are neither perfect nor evil nor entirely innocent: instead, they come much closer to the Aristotelian concept of the hero afflicted with *hamartia* (a tragic flaw). They are all driven by passions they cannot control: pride forces them to seek revenge, ambition makes them long to wage an unjust war, erotic desire moves them to court an unobtainable lady, or jealousy leads them to their eventual downfall. Many of the characters are heroes with these tragic flaws, but heroes just the same in their battle against the rational world whose rules they can understand but by which they cannot live.

In these cases the devices of foreshadowing are not used merely to excite an emotional response from the audience, but rather to force the protagonist to foresee some of the consequences of his actions, and gain a greater awareness of his own motives. At the same time the protagonist's passion is invariably greater than his willingness to face the truth of his situation, so he talks himself into ignoring the warning of the so-called voice of fate which comes to him in the guise of foreshadowing. His self-deception is only partly successful, however, for although he chooses to follow his passion, he cannot deny that his mind has registered the warning.

We encountered two exceptions where lovers were able to renounce their passion when we discussed *La Santa Liga* and *Las paces de los reyes,* but generally the lovers become tragic figures who foresee the consequences of their passion, yet are unable to come to terms with their inevitable destiny. The best examples of such lovers are examined in Part Three in the sections dealing with *La imperial de Otón* and *El caballero de Olmedo.*

The protagonist who has foreknowledge of his destiny (but is powerless to change it) has all the makings of a tragic figure, providing, of course, he meets the Aristotelian standards of character. But when he is unaware of the meaning and inevitable consequences of his feelings and behavior, he becomes an ironic figure whose actions and false expectations inspire pity and fear in the spectators whose vision and understanding is deeper than that of the protagonist.

Self-awareness, however, cannot always be successfully blanketed by self-deception and rationalizations, so the character is almost invariably disturbed by inner conflicts resulting from the clash between his foreknowledge and his desire not to know. To the extent that he truly knows less than the spectators, then, he is an ironic figure; but to the extent that he is aware of what lies ahead yet is unable or unwilling to do anything about it, he is a tragic figure whose destiny is foreseen both by him and the by spectators as well.

There is often a sort of overlapping of ironic and tragic qualities in the character of the protagonist, but we see, in the case of Otón, for example, that there is a specific moment of *anagnōrisis* when he is forced by the silent *sombra* to recognize the underlying truth of his situation. He sees beyond the immediate problem of his own passion, and perceives, at last, both the nobility and the absurdity of human strivings (this is well illustrated in his speech with the refrain *y todo por una mujer*—"and all for a woman").

Lope's characters as they appear in Part Three are often brought to their moment of recognition as a result of this graphically symbolic form of self-confrontation with the silent *sombra,* which is seen by the hero as a representation of himself (or an extension of his own being), and the experience fills him with dread and foreboding, brought about by his self-knowledge and his loss of innocence. From that moment on he begins to lose his identity as ironic dupe, and acquires the tragic dimensions of the hero who knows, but cannot accept or even admit his knowledge.

The majority of the omens, dreams, and prophecies in Lope's plays come true, serving as guideposts to point the way to the an exciting outcome. These devices, coupled with the literary foreshadowing inherent in the many popular themes that Lope chooses to dramatize (biblical, historical, epic, mythological, and motifs drawn from ballads) make most of the endings foreseeable, but the spectators are taken on an breathtaking ride as they view the developing destinies of villains, victims, lovers, heroes, royalty, bawds, shadows and other figures both tragic and comic. The interaction of these passionate and often conflicted characters have kept Lope's audiences enthralled for half a millenium, and will no doubt continue to do so for a very long time to come.

APPENDIX

Alphabetical list of plays mentioned in this book:

*Adonis y Venus**[137]*
*almenas de Toro, Las**
amante agradecido, El
amigo por fuerza, El
anzuelo de Fenisa, El
arauco domado, El
arenal de Sevilla, El
asalto de Mastrique, El
Barlaán y Josafat
bastardo Mudarra, El
bella Aurora, La
bella malmaridada, La
buena guarda, La
Castelvines y Monteses
castigo del discreto, El
castigo sin venganza, El
comedia de Bamba, La
*comendadores de Córdoba, Los**
conde Fernán González, El
Contra valor no hay desdicha
marido más firme, El
marqués de Mantua, El
marqués de las Navas, El
más galán portugués, El

creación del mundo, La[138]
cuerdo loco, El
desdichada Estefanía, La
*divino africano, El**
Don Juan de Castro I
Don Juan de Castro II
duque de Viseo, El
*fingido verdadero, Lo**
francesilla, La
Fuente Ovejuna
ganso de oro, El
Hamete de Toledo, El
hermosa Ester, La
hijo de los leones, El
imperial de Otón, La
inocente sangre, La
justas de Tebas, Las
Laura perseguida
Lo que está determinado
Lo que ha de ser
piadoso veneciano, El
Porfiar hasta morir
premio de la hermosura, El
príncipe despeñado, El

---

[137] The plays followed by asterisks contain examples of specific devices of foreshadowing, but since they did not add anything new to the plays already discussed in this book, I did not include them in the text.
[138] Authorship questioned by Morley and Bruerton

mayordomo de la duquesa
	de Amalfi, El*
mejor mozo de España, El
montañesa, La*
niño inocente de la Guardia, El
nueva victoria del marqués
	de Santa Cruz, La*
nuevo mundo descubierto por
	Cristóbal Colón, El
paces de los reyes, Las
Pedro Carbonero
Peribáñez
piadoso aragonés, El

príncipe perfecto I, El
príncipe perfecto II, El
Ramírez de Arellano, Los
robo de Dina, El
rufián Castrucho, El
Santa Liga, La
serrana de la Vera, La
servir con mala estrella, El
trabajos de Jacob, Los
tragedia del rey don
	Sebastián, La
último godo, El

The following is a brief summary of the plays with asterisks not mentioned in the body of this book:

Adonis y Venus: Apollo's prophecies to the various lovers end up coming true; Adonis dreams that his life will come to an end just before he meets his death.

Las almenas de Toro: The Cid tells Sancho that if he goes against his father's will, he will be cursed with his malediction. The traitor Bellido Dolfos kills Sancho, thus fulfilling the malediction.

Los comendadores de Córdoba: A popular ballad with sad overtones is sung in Act Three. The *comendadores* are beset with bad omens: Fernando could not unsheath his sword, a mirror shatters, Jorge's reins break, he hears a dog barking, he falls, their horses fight and one kicks the other to death. Both *comendadores* have nightmares, and one hears a blood-curdling scream. The *Veinticuatro* kills them, his wife, the maids, the dog, the cats, the parrot, and the monkey.

El divino africano: The progagonist's mother's dream comes true: an angel tells her that her son, Agustín, will become a Christian. His wife's prediction also comes true: she compares herself to Dido, who loses Aeneas. She does lose him; he remains in Italy and finally becomes a saint.

Lo fingido verdadero: A voice tells Ginés that he will become a Christian; the prediction comes true. There are infinite opportunities to point out ironies in this Pirandello-like play. Ginés mysteriously foresees everything, for he writes the plays which ultimately come true. (This play was omitted because it requires very special treatment.)

El mayordomo de la duquesa de Amalfi: The maid's prediction comes true: Libia tells the Duchess that her love for the caretaker will cause their death because of their *desigualdad* (inequality). Actually there is amazingly little foreshadowing considering the wholesale massacre that occurs at the end.

La montañesa: The Roman consul's prediction comes true: he tells the villain Andronio that he will die for the love of a slave.

La nueva victoria del marqués de Santa Cruz: The *hechicera* Dalifa's prophecy comes true: she foresees a great victory for Santa Cruz. There is a good speech about her not being able to change the decrees of the heavens.

Chronological list of plays containing specific foreshadowing (dates taken from Morley and Bruerton):

El ganso de oro	(1588-1595)
La tragedia del rey don Sebastán	(1593-1603)
Las justas de Tebas	(before 1596)
Los comendadores de Córdoba	(1596-1598)
La comedia de Bamba	(1597-1598)
La imperial de Otón	(1598?)
Adonis y Venus	(1597-1603)
La Santa Liga	(1598-1600?)
El nuevo mundo descubierto por	
Cristóbal Colón	(1598?-1603)
El arauco domado	(1599?)
El último godo	(1599-1603)
El amigo por fuerza	(1599-1603)
El príncipe despeñado	(1602)
El marqués de Mantua	(1600?-1602?)
La montañesa	(Before 1604)
La nueva victoria del marqués	
de Santa Cruz	(1604)
El mayordomo de la duquesa de Amalfi	(1604-1606)
Don Juan de Castro, I	(1597-1608)
La desdichada Estefanía	(1604)
El servir con mala estrella	(1604?-1606?)
Los Ramírez de Arellano	(1604-1608)
La inocente sangre	(1604-1608)
Lo fingido verdadero	(1608?)
El duque de Viseo	(1608?-1609?)
La hermosa Ester	(1610)

El Hamete de Toledo	(1610?)
El divino africano	(1610?)
El mejor mozo de España	(1610-1611)
Las paces de los reyes	(1610-1612)
El conde Fernán González	(1610-1612)
Las almenas de Toro	(1610-1613?)
El premio de la hermosura	(1610-1615)
El bastardo Mudarra	(1612)
El príncipe perfecto I	(1614?)
Lo que está determinado	(1613-1619)
El robo de Dina	(1615-1622)
El marido más firme	(1620-1621)
El caballero de Olmedo	(1620?-1625?)
Los trabajos de Jacob	(1620-1630)
El marqués de las Navas	(1624)
Lo que ha de ser	(1626)
El piadoso aragonés	(1626)
Contra valor no hay desdicha	(1625?-1630?)

A glance at the chronological list indicates that there is very little significant change from one decade to the next in the number of plays having specific devices of foreshadowing. It is, of course, difficult to fit the plays into definitive, clearly-defined decades, since their dates cannot always be ascertained with accuracy. One can nevertheless get an idea of the approximate number belonging to each decade by averaging the outside dates of the plays whose dates are uncertain (*i.e.*, for the sake of convenience, a play dated 1618-1622 could be considered 1620). In this way we find that ten plays written before 1600 contain devices of foreshadowing; seventeen between 1601 and 1610; nine from 1611 to 1620; and seven from 1620 on. If we then count the authentic plays listed by

Morley and Bruerton we find there are 65 in the first period,
112 in the second, 83 in the third, and 44 in the last. This the
third, and 16% in the last. The following chart should clarify
the matter:

	Plays with devices of foreshadowing:	Total number of authentic plays:	Ratios
-1600:	10	65	15%
1601-1610:	17	112	15%
1611-1620:	9	83	11%
1621-	7	44	16%

Lope seems to have been just slightly less interested in using
devices of foreshadowing in the period 1611-1620. While it
is true that I have only checked 70 of the entire group of 304
authentic plays, it is nevertheless a large enough sampling to
allow us to draw the conclusion that Lope's interest in foreshadowing seems to have persisted throughout the entire corpus of his plays.

Chronological lists of the types of foreshadowing:

Vocal *sombras*

El ganso de oro	(1588-1595)
El arauco domado	(1599?)
Don Juan de Castro, I	(1597-1608)
El duque de Viseo	(1608?-1609?)
El premio de la hermosura	(1610-1615)
El príncipe perfecto, I	(1614?)
El marqués de las Navas	(1624)
Contra valor no hay desdicha	(1625?-1630?)

Silent *sombras*

Las justas de Tebas	(before 1596)
La imperial de Otón	(1598?)
La Santa Liga	(1598-1600)
Las paces de los reyes	(1610-1612)
El robo de Dina	(1615-1625?)
El caballero de Olmedo	(1620?-1625?)

Omens

Los comendadores de Córdoba	(1596-1598)
La imperial de Otón	(1598?)
El último godo	(1599-1603)
El arauco domado	(1599?)
El marqués de Mantua	(1600?-1602?)
La desdichada Estefanía	(1604)
El Hamete de Toledo	(1610?)
El mejor mozo de España	(1610-1611)
Las paces de los reyes	(1610-1612)
El bastardo Mudarra	(1612)
El marido más firme	(1620-1621)
El caballero de Olmedo	(1620?-1625?)
Contra valor no hay desdicha	(1625?-1630?)

Dreams (prophetic)

El ganso de oro	(1588-1595)
La hermosa Ester	(1610)
El divino africano	(1610?)
El mejor mozo de España	(1610-1611)
Lo que está determinado	(1613-1619)
Los trabajos de Jacob	(1620-1630)

Dreams (nightmares)

Los comendadores de Córdoba	(1596-1598)
La comedia de Bamba	(1597-1598)
Adonis y Venus	(1597-1603)
El amigo por fuerza	(1599-1603)
El último godo	(1599-1603)
La inocente sangre	(1604-1608)
El bastardo Mudarra	(1612)

Prophecies

La tragedia del rey don Sebastián	(1593-1603)
La comedia de Bamba	(1597-1598)
Adonis y Venus	(1597-1603)
El nuevo mundo descubierto por Cristóbal Colón	(1598?-1603)
El arauco domado	(1599?)
El último godo	(1599-1603)
La nueva victoria del marqués de Santa Cruz	(1604)
La desdichada Estefanía	(1604)
Los Ramírez de Arellano	(1604-1608)
El Hamete de Toledo	(1610?)
El conde Fernán González	(1610-1612)
Las almenas de Toro	(1610-1613?)
El marido más firme	(1620-1621)
Lo que ha de ser	(1624)
El piadoso aragonés	(1626)
Contra valor no hay desdicha	(1625?-1630?)

In examining the types of foreshadowing that Lope de Vega used in his plays, we find he had no particular predilection for any one of them. Fourteen *sombras* made an appearance in the seventy plays that were studied, thirteen omens were acknowledged, sixteen prophecies were uttered, and thirteen dreams were dreamed. Again we see that these devices were distributed fairly evenly throughout Lope's opus; the only noteworthy absences being the disappearance after 1612 of prophetic nightmares of death and violence, and a total lack of silent *sombras* in the period 1601-1610.

When I first undertook the organization of this thesis, I secretly hoped to discover some indication of a progression from the less interesting devices of foreshadowing to those having a much greater dramatic value. I thought that perhaps the prosaic, long-winded vocal *sombras* would eventually give way to the mysterious silent *sombras* that appeared at the moment of the protagonist's greatest emotional crisis and often represented his new and terrible self-recognition and clairvoyance. But no, *la imperial de Otón,* a play comparable to *El caballero de Olmedo* in depth and scope, was written around 1598, and *El marqués de las Navas,* which presented us with one of the most tedious ghost scenes in Lope's entire repertoire, appeared in 1624.

This only proves what we already know about Lope's erratic genius; he wrote constantly, and just about every play was designed to appeal in one way or another to his insatiable audience's taste for any sort of theatrical trick that would astonish or entertain them. He wrote plays as fast as he could, and many of them turned out to be masterpieces. Others, however, were bound to fail, but there were very few that did not in some way reflect his acute observation of customs and manners, his natural and spontaneous talent for composing verse, and his altogether unique ability to create characters with a special *gracia,* or Lopean charm.

LIST OF WORKS CONSULTED

AESCHYLUS, *Prometheus Bound, the Complete Greek Tragedies* (vol. I), ed. David Grene and Richard Lattimore, N.Y. (Random House), n.d.

ALONSO, DÁMASO, "Tres procesos de dramatización," *De los siglos oscuros al de oro,* Madrid (Gredos), 1958, 144-147.

ANDERSON IMBERT, ENRIQUE, "Lope dramatiza un cantar," in *Crítica interna,* Madrid, 1960, 17-18.

ANÍBAL, C. E., *"Voces del Cielo*: A Note on Mira de Amescua", *RR,* XVI (1925), 57-70.

— "Another Note on the *Voces del Cielo:* A Note on Mira de Amescua," *RR,* XVIII (1927), 246-252.

ARCO Y GARAY, RICARDO DEL, *La sociedad española en las obras dramáticas de Lope de Vega,* Madrid, 1941.

ARISTOTLE, *Poetics,* translation Ingram Bywater, N.Y. (Random House), 1954.

AUBRUN, CHARLES V., "Inventaire des sources pour l'étude de la poésie castillane du quinzième siècle", *Estudios dedicados a Menéndez Pidal,* IV (1953), 297-330.

— "La *comedia* doctrinale et ses histoires de brigands: *El condenado por desconfiado*", *BH,* LIX (1957), 137-151.

— "La *Comédie Espagnole (1600-1680),* Publications de la Faculté des Lettres et Sciences Humaines de Paris, Sorbonne Série "Études et Méthodes", tome 14. Presses Universitaires de France, Paris, 1966.

AVALLE-ARCE, JUAN B., *La novela pastoril española,* Madrid, 1959.

BABBITT, IRVING, *Rousseau and Romanticism* (1919), Ohio (Meridian Books), 1966.

BATAILLON, MARCEL, *Erasmo y España,* Mexico, 1966. (First published as *Erasme el l'Espagne,* Paris, 1937.)
— *"La Célestine" selon Fernando de Rojas,* Paris, 1961.
BENAVENTE, MANUEL, *Los amores de Lope de Vega,* San José (Uruguay), Ed. Cenit, 1949.
BERNDT, ERNA RUTH, *Amor, muerte, y fortuna en "La Celestina,"* Madrid, 1963.
BIRNEY, EARLE, "English Irony Before Chaucer," *University of Toronto Quarterly,* VI, #4 (1937), 538-557.
CAMUS, ALBERT, Introduction to *Le Chevalier d'Olmedo,* Paris, 1957.
CAPELLANUS, ANDREAS, *The Art of Courtly Love,* trans. John Jay Parry, New York, 1959.
CASA, FRANK, "The Dramtic Unity of *El caballero de Olmedo,*" *Neophilologus,* V (1966), 234-243.
CASALDUERO, J., *Estudios sobre el teatro español,* Madrid, 1962.
CASTRO, AMÉRICO, "Algunas observaciones acerca del concepto del honor en los siglos XVI y XVII", *RFE,* III (1916), 1-50.
— *La realidad histórica de España,* Mexico, 1954.
— *De la edad conflictiva,* Madrid, 1961.
CHAYTOR, H. J., *Dramatic Theory in Spain: Extracts from Literature Before and During the Golden Age,* Cambridge, 1925.
CIRUELO, PEDRO, *Reprobación de las supersticiones y hechicerías* (1530), Madrid, 1952.
DE ROUGEMONT, DENIS, *Love in the Western World,* New York, 1957.
— *Love Declared: Essays on the Myths of Love,* New York (Random House), 1963.
DYSON, A. E., *The Crazy Fabric: Essays in Irony,* London (Macmillan), 1965.

EDWARDS, GWYNNE, *Lope de Vega: Three Major Plays: Fuente Ovejuna, The Knight from Olmedo, Punishment Without Revenge.* Oxford University Press, N.Y. 2008. Translations, Introduction, and notes by G. Edwards.

ENTRAMBASAGUAS, JOAQUÍN DE, *Una guerra literaria del siglo de oro: Lope de Vega y los preceptistas aristotélicos,* Madrid, 1932.

EURIPIDES, *Hippolytus, The Complete Greek Tragedies,* (vol. 5), Ed. David Greene and Richmond Lattimore, New York (Random House), n.d.

FARINELLI, ARTURO, *La vita é un sogno* (2 vols.) Turin, 1929.

— *Lope de Vega en Alemania,* Barcelona, 1936.

FERGUSSON, FRANCIS, *The Idea of a Theatre,* Princeton Univ. Press, 1949.

FERRER, ORLANDO, "El gran amor de Lope de Vega", *Revista Cubana,* III (1935), 186-229.

FICHTER, W. L., *Lope de Vega's "El castigo del discreto" Together with a Study of Conjugal Honor in his Theatre,* New York, 1925.

FOSTER, DAVID WILLIAM, "Some Attitudes Towards Love in *La Celestina,*" *Hispania,* XLVIII (1965), 484-492.

FOWLIE, WALLACE, *Love in Literature,* New York, 1965.

FREUD, SIGMUND, *Beyond the Pleasure Principle* (1920), London (Hogarth Press), 1955.

FROLDI, RINALDO, *Lope de Vega y la formación de la Comedia,* Salamanca (Anaya), 1968.

GAOS, VICENTE, *Temas y problemas de literatura española,* (chapter entitled "La poética invisible de Lope de Vega"), Madrid, 1959.

GÉRARD, ALBERT S., "Baroque Unity and the Dualities of *El Caballero de Olmedo," RR,* LVI (1965), 92-106.

GILMAN, STEPHEN, *The Art of "La Celestina,"* Madison (Univ. of Wisconsin Press), 1956.

GLASER, EDWARD, "Lope de Vega's *El niño inocente de la Guardia,*" *BHS,* XXXII (1955), 140-153.

GONZÁLEZ DE AMEZÚA, Agustín, *Lope de Vega en sus cartas. Introducción al epistolario de Lope de Vega Carpio* (4 vols.) Madrid, 1935-1943.

The Great Ideas: A Syntopicon of Great Books of the Western World (vol. II), Robert Maynard Hutchins, Ed.-in-Chief, Encyclopedia Britannica, Inc., 1952.

GREEN, OTIS H., "Courtly Love in the Spanish Cancioneros," *PMLA,* LXIV (1949), 247-301.

— *Spain and the Western Tradition* (4 vols.), Madison, 1963-1968.

GRISMER, RAYMOND L., *Bibliography of Lope de Vega* (2 vols.), Minneapolis, 1965.

HALSTEAD, FRANK G., "The Attitude of Lope de Vega toward Astrology and Astronomy," *HR,* VII (1939), 205-219.

HEILMON, ROBERT, "Tragedy and Melodrama: Speculations on Generic Form," *Texas Quarterly,* III (1960), 36-50.

HERMENEGILDO, ALFREDO, *Los trágicos españoles del siglo XVI,* Madrid, 1961.

HERRERO, MIGUEL, and Manuel Cardenal, "Sobre lo agüeros en la literatura española del Siglo de Oro", *RFE,* XXVI (1942), 15-41.

HESSE, EVERETT W., "The Role of the Mind in Lope's *El Caballero de Olmedo,*" Symposium, XIX (1965), 58-66.

— *Análisis e interpretación de la Comedia,* Madrid (Castalia) 1968.

HIERRO, JOSÉ, "Algunos aspectos del teatro del Siglo de Oro", *Bolívar* (Caracas), No. 45 (Nov./Dec., 1955), 865-874.

HIGHET, GILBERT, *The Classical Tradition: Greek and Roman Influences on Western Literature,* N. Y., 1965 (first published by Oxford University Press, 1949).

JEBB, SIR RICHARD, "The Genius of Sophocles," *Essays and Addresses,* Cambridge (1907), 29-33.

KNOX, NORMAN, *The Word "Irony" and its Context, 1500-1755,* Durham, N.C. (Duke Univ. Press), 1961

LEWIS, C. S., *The Allegory of Love: A Study of Medieval Tradition* (1936), New York, 1958.

LUCAS, F. L. *Tragedy* (1927), N. Y. (Collier Books), 1957.

MacCURDY, RAYMOND R., *Francisco de Rojas y Zorilla and the Tragedy,* Albuquerque, 1958.

MALKIEL, MARÍA ROSA LIDA DE, *Introducción al teatro de Sófocles,* Buenos Aires, 1944.

— *La originalidad artística de la Celestina,* Buenos Aires, 1962.

— *Dos obras maestras españolas: "El libro de buen amor" y "La Celestina",* Buenos Aires, 1966.

MANDEL, OSCAR, *A Definition of Tragedy,* New York (N.Y. University Press), 1961.

MARAVALL, JOSÉ ANTONIO, *El mundo social de "La Celestina",* Madrid (Gredos), 1964.

MARÍN, DIEGO, *La intriga secundaria en el teatro de Lope de Vega,* Mexico, 1958.

— "La ambigüedad dramática en *El caballero de Olmedo", Hispanófila,* XXIV (1965) 1-11.

MARTÍNEZ DE TOLEDO, ALFONSO, *El arcipreste de Talavera,* Intro. and notes by Mario Penna, Turin, n.d.

MAY, ROLLO, *Love and Will,* New York, 1969.

McCRARY, WILLIAM C., *"Fuenteovejuna:* Its Platonic Vision and Execution," *Studies in Philology,* LVIII, 1961.

— *The Goldfinch and the Hawk: A Study of Lope de Vega*'s *"El Caballero de Olmedo",* Chapel Hill (Univ. of N. C. Press), 1966.

McCREADY, WARREN T., *Bibliografía temática de estudios sobre el teatro español antiguo,* Toronto, 1966.

McFARLAND, THOMAS, *Tragic Meanings in Shakespeare,* N.Y. (Random House), 1966.

McLAUGHLIN, PETER, "The Elements of Tragedy", *Queen's Quarterly*, LXXI (1964), 103-111.

MENÉNDEZ Y PELAYO, MARCELINO, *Histora de las ideas estéticas en España*, Madrid, 1883-1891. (5 vols.)

— *Orígines de la novela*, (*NBAE* I, VII, XIV, XXI), Madrid, 1905-1915.

— *Estudios sobre el teatro de Lope de Vega*, Madrid, 1919-1927. (6 vols.)

— *Historia de los heterodoxos españoles*, Santander, 1947. (Vols. 35-42 of *Obras completas*, Ed. Enrique Sánchez Reyes).

MENÉNDEZ PIDAL, RAMÓN, *La epopeya castellana a través de la literatura española*, 2nd ed., Buenos Aires, 1945.

— *De Cervantes y Lope de Vega*, Madrid (Austral), 1940.

MILLÉ Y JIMÉNEZ, JUAN, "El horóscopo de Lope de Vega", *Humanidades* (La Plata, Argentina), XV (1927), 69-96.

MOIR, DUNCAN, "The Classical Tradition in Spanish Dramatic Theory and Practice in the Seventeenth Century". In *Classical Drama and Its Influence. Essays Presented to H.D.F. Kitto*, ed. M.J. Anderson, London (1965), 193- 228.

MONTESINOS, JOSÉ F., study accompanying *La corona merecida, TAE*, V (1925), p. 155 ff.

— Introduction to *El cuerdo loco, TAE*, IV (1925).

— Introduction to *El marqués de las Navas, TAE*, VI (1925), pp. 138-168.

— *Estudios sobre Lope de Vega*, Mexico (El colegio de Mexico), 1951.

— "La paradoja del *Arte Nuevo*," *RO*, V (1965), 302-330.

MORBY, EDWIN S., "Some observations on *Tragedia* and *Tragicomedia* in Lope", *HR*, XI (1943), 185-209.

MORLEY GRISWOLD, and COURTNEY BRUERTON, *The Chronology of Lope de Vega's "Comedias"*, London, 1940.

— "Addenda to *The Chronology of Lope de Vega's "Comedias"*, *HR*, XV (1947), 49-71.

MYERS, HENRY ALONZO, *Tragedy, a View of Life*, Cornell University Press, 1956.

NAGY, EDWARD, *Lope de Vega y "La Celestina"*: *Perspectiva pseudocelestinesca en las comedias de Lope*, Cuadernos de la Facultad de Filosofía, Letras, y Ciencias (no. 39), Mexico, 1968.

NIETZSCHE, FRIEDRICH, *The Birth of Tragedy* (1872), trans. Walter Kaufman, N.Y. (Random House), 1967.

OLIVER ASÍN, J., "Más reminiscencias de *La Celestina* en el teatro de Lope," *RFE*, SV (1928), 67-74.

OLSON, ELDER, *Tragedy and the Theory of Drama*, Detroit (Wayne State Univ. Press), 1966.

ORTEGA Y GASSET, JOSÉ, *Estudios sobre el amor*, Madrid (Revista de Occidente), 1957. (first ed.: 1940)

OVID, *The Art of Love*, translation Rolfo Humphries, Bloomington (Indiana Univ. Press), 1957.

— *Metamorphoses* (2 vols.), trans. Frank Justus Miller, Loeb Classical Library, Cambridge (Harvard University Press), 1960 (first ed. 1916).

PARKER, A. A., "The Approach to the Spanish Drama of the Golden Age," *TDR*, IV (1959), 42-59.

PARKER, J. H., *Breve historia del teatro español*, Mexico, 1957.

PARKER, JACK H. and ARTHUR M. FOX, eds., *Lope de Vega Studies, 1937-1962: A Critical Survey and Annotated Bibliography*, University of Toronto Press, 1964.

PÉREZ, LUÍS, and F. SÁNCHEZ ESCRIBANO, *Afirmaciones de Lope de Vega sobre la perspectiva dramática*, Madrid, 1961.

PEYRE, HENRI, "The Tragedy of Passion: Racine's *Phèdre*." In *Tragic Themes in Western Literature*, New Haven (Yale Univ. Press), 1955.

REICHENBERGER, ARNOLD G., "The Uniqueness of the *Comedia*," *HR,* XXVII (1959), 303-316.

REIK, THEODOR, *Of Love and Lust,* N.Y., 1968. (first edition 1941).

RENNERT, HUGO ALBERT, *The Spanish Stage in the Time of Lope de Vega,* N.Y. (Dover), 1963.

— and AMÉRICO CASTRO, *Vida de Lope de Vega,* Madrid (1918), new ed. Salamanca (Anaya), 1968.

RICO, FRANCISCO, *"El caballero de Olmedo:* muerte, amor, ironía," *Papeles de Son Armadans,* XLVII, no. cxxxix, Oct. 1967, 38-56.

— Introduction to *El caballero de Olmedo,* Salamanca (Anaya), 1968.

RODRÍGUEZ MOÑINO, A., *El Cancionero General* (Valencia 1511; Anvers 1573) *Noticias bibliográficas...,* Madrid, 1958.

ROJAS, FERNANDO DE, *La Celestina* (Introduction by Stephen Gilman, ed. and notes by Dorothy Severin), Madrid, 1969.

ROMERA-NAVARRO, M., *La preceptiva dramática de Lope de Vega y otros ensayos sobre el Fénix,* Madrid, 1935.

RUGG, EVYLYN, "El padre en el teatro de Lope de Vega," *Hispanófila,* XXV (1965), 1-16.

RUGGERIO, MICHAEL J., *The Evolution of the Go-Between in Spanish Literature Through the Sixteenth Century,* Univ. of California Pubs. in Modern Philology, 78, 1966.

RUIZ RAMÓN, F., *Historia del teatro español,* Madrid, 1967.

SCHEVILL, RUDOLPH, *The Dramatic Art of Lope de Vega: with "La dama boba",* Berkeley, 1915.

SCHLEGEL, A.W., *Course in Dramatic Literature,* London, 1815.

SEDGEWICK, G. G., *Of Irony, Especially in Drama,* Toronto (Univ. of Toronto Press), 1935.

SEWALL, RICHARD B., *The Vision of Tragedy,* New
    Haven (Yale Univ. Press), 1959.
SHARPE, ROBERT BOIES, *Irony in the Drama: an Essay
    on Impersonation, Shock, and Catharsis,* Chapel Hill
    (Univ. of N.C. Press), 1959.
SHEPARD, SANFORD, *El Pinciano y las teorías literarias
    del Siglo de Oro,* Madrid, 1962.
SHERGOLD, N. D., *A History of the Spanish Stage,* Oxford,
    1967.
SIMÓN DÍAZ, JOSÉ, and JUANA DE JOSÉ PRADES,
    *Ensayo de una bibliografía de las obras y artículos
    sobre la vida y escritos de Lope de Vega Carpio,*
    Madrid, 1955.
SOONS, ALAN, "Towards an Intepretation of *El caballero
    de Olmedo*", *RF,* 73 (1961), 160-168.
SOULE, DONALD E., *Irony in Early Critical Comedy,*
    Unpub. doct. diss., Stanford, 1959.
SPITZER, LEO, "A Central Theme and its Structural
    Equivalent in Lope's *Fuente Ovejuna*", *HR,* XXIII
    (1955).
STENDHAL, *De l'amour* (1822), Paris, 1957.
THIRLWALL, BISHOP CONNOP, "On the Irony of
    Sophocles", *Philological Museum,* II (1833), 483-537.
THOMPSON, A. R., *The Dry Mock: a Study of Irony in the
    Drama,* (Univ. of Calif. Press), 1948.
THOMSON, J. A. K., *Irony, an Historical Introduction,*
    Cambridge (Harvard Univ. Press), 1927.
TRISTAN AND ISEULT, as retold by Joseph Bédier, New
    York (Doubleday), 1945. First published in France,
    1900.
TRUEBLOOD ALAN B., *Substance and Form in "La
    Dorotea". A Study in Lope's Artistic Use of Personal
    Experience.* Unpub. doct. diss., Harvard University,
    1951.
— "Role-playing and the Sense of Illusion in Lope de
    Vega", *HR* XXXII (1964), 305-318.

TURNER, ALISON, "The Dramatic Function of Imagery and Symbolism in *Peribáñez* and *El caballero de Olmedo*", *Symposium*, XX (1966), 174-186.

UNAMUNO, MIGUEL DE, *Del sentimiento trágico de la vida*, Madrid, 1937.

VALBUENA PRAT, ANGEL, *Historia del teatro español*, Barcelona 1956.

VEGA Y CARPIO, LOPE FÉLIX DE, *Obras de Lope de Vega* (15 vols.), publicadas por la Real Academia Española, ed. M. Menéndez y Pelayo, Madrid, 1890-1913.

— *Obras de Lope de Vega* (13 vols.), publicadas por la Real Academia Española (Nueva Edición), ed. Emilio Cotarelo y Mori, Madrid, 1916-1930.

VILLANOVA, A., "Preceptistas españolas de los siglos XVI y XVII", in *Historia general de las literaturas hispánicas*, III, Barcelona, 1953.

VOSSLER, KARL, *Lope de Vega y su tiempo*, trans. Ramón de la Serna, 2nd ed., Madrid, 1940.

YATES, D. A., "The Poetry of the Fantastic in *El caballero de Olmedo*", *H*, XLIII (1960), 503-507.

INDEX

eirōn, 17, 89, 90

Farinelli, Arturo, (footnotes: pp. 94, 134)

fate, 12-15, 18, 21, 22, 26, 28, 31, 39, 43, 48, 51, 52, 54, 58, 60, 69, 70, 79, 88, 97, 98, 100, 103, 110, 119, 126, 137, 138, 140, 145, 157, 164, 166, 168, 170-172, (footnote pp. 61, 68, 75)

foreknowledge, 12, 14, 18, 26-28, 31, 39, 40-42, 53, 54, 58, 62, 72, 78, 83, 85, 88-90, 112, 122, 126, 137, 173, (footnote pp. 68, 78)

foresee(ing), 11, 18, 28, 38, 41, 55, 60, 69, 79-83, 85, 88-90, 92, 98, 106, 110, 114, 136, 145, 151, 162, 171-174, 177

foreshadow(ing), 9, 11-14, 22, 25-30, 32, 36, 41, 42, 53, 55, 56, 60, 62, 64, 69-71, 79, 81, 85, 89, 94, 99, 102, 103, 105, 111, 117, 121, 123, 124, 126, 139, 140, 144,149, 150, 159, 160, 171, 172, 174, 177, 179, 180, 182, 183, (footnotes: pp. 37, 175)

free will (see also determinism), 8, 13, 26, 28, 87, 88, 91, 93, 95, 98, (footnotes: pp. 71, 87)

Freud, Sigmund, 99, 186, (footnote: p. 100)

ghost(s), 7, 11, 12, 25-27, 30-33, 36-42, 52, 72, 106, 110-112, 116, 132, 145, 164, 165, 183, (foot: pp. 100, 132, 168)

Gilman, Stephen, 5, 6, 186, 191

Green, Otis, 65, 100, (footnotes: pp. 24, 45, 47, 65, 75, 99, 100, 142, 145)

God's will, 53, 60, 62, 75, 97, 167 (footnotes: pp. 65, 75, 90)

hamartia, 21, 22, 172

Halstead, Frank, 187, (footnotes: pp. 26, 116)

Herrero, Miguel, 187, (footnote: p. 44)

honor(able), 31, 32, 34, 38, 39, 42, 47, 48, 50, 58, 59, 60, 72, 109, 111, 112, 115, 120, 122, 125, 126, 129, 130, 134, 135, 137, 139, 140, 148, 158, 165, 185, 186, (footnote: pp. 50, 51)

hubris, 79, 104, 123, 129, (footnote: p. 17)

ironic devices, 15

ironic distance, 12, 79, 85, 105

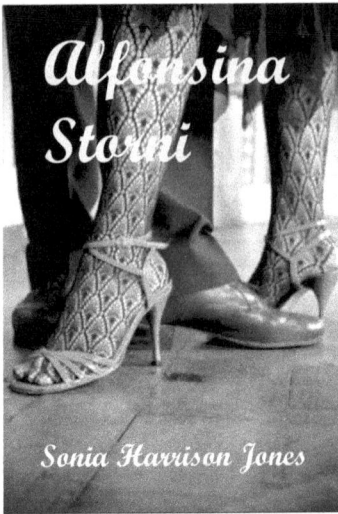

Alfonsina Storni was an important poet, playwright and journalist in Latin America during the 20th century. Born in Switzerland and raised in Argentina, she was a major force in the Modernist and feminist movements. Sonia Harrison Jones was awarded a Canada Council grant to research Storni's publications in Buenos Aires, where she combed through archives and also interviewed most of the literati who had known the poet. Dr. Jones provides thoughtful, valuable insights into Storni's turbulent life and expressive opus.

WHAT READERS ARE SAYING

"It is remarkable that this book, written in 1979, was still a best seller on Amazon in 2003." —Claudia Edith Mendez, PhD thesis, University of Maryland

"Sonia (Harrison) Jones is one of the pioneering scholars in bringing attention to the importance of Storni's contribution to the feminist movement." —Celia Garzón-Arrabal, "The Theater of Alfonsina Storni: Feminism and Innovation" ProQuest, 2008 (PhD thesis, University of North Carolina, Chapel Hill)

This is one of four books on the reading list for Latin American Women's Poetry at Cambridge University's Faculty of Modern & Medieval Languages.

Available on Amazon or at www.erserandpond.com

Spanish One

Sonia Harrison Jones

Spanish One Workbook

Sonia Harrison Jones

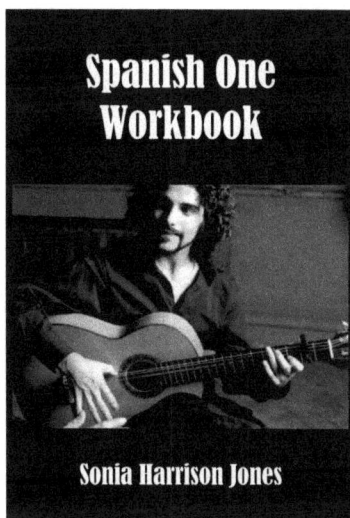

This is a beginning Spanish university-level textbook. The author, who has published novels, a biography, a memoir and many humor articles for *The Banner* and *The Reader's Digest,* makes this textbook enjoyable for students by including a cast of fictional characters who are studying at a university in Nova Scotia.

She also makes it possible for real life, non-fictional students to develop their Spanish vocabulary quickly by providing many cognates which she incorporates into both the reading material and the exercises. She places a strong emphasis on grammar in her textbook, since most adults, unlike children, do not readily absorb languages by osmosis.

Dr. Jones has created stories and excercises throughout the textbook and the workbook to help illustrate the grammar concepts and to provide the students with a constant opportunity to practice what they have learned. A CD is also included in the package to help the students accomplish this purpose.

Available on Amazon or at www.erserandpond.com

www.ingramcontent.com/pod-product-compliance
Lightning Source LLC
Chambersburg PA
CBHW060922040426
42445CB00011B/748